CW00545202

REBEL VEGAN TRAVEL GUIDE

VEGANISM ON THE GO

TODD SINCLAIR

First published 2021 by Intrepid Fox Publishing Ltd

20-22 Wenlock Road
London N1 7GU

Hardback ISBN 978-1-7398490-8-5
Paperback ISBN 978-1-7398490-7-8
eISBN 978-1-7398490-6-1

REBELVEGANLIFE.COM

Original Illustrations by Cathy Brear
Recipe Development by Lara Schirkhorschidi

Other Images by Shutterstock

To all those who wander,
You have a home here

Exclusive Thank You Gift
for Rebel Vegan Readers:
FREE Download of Complimentary ebook

TOP 10 VEGAN SUPERFOODS
With Nutritional Guidelines and Recipes

https://rebelveganlife.ck.page/rebelvegansuperfoods

CONTENTS

INTRODUCTION

ALL ABOARD: WELCOME TO VEGAN TRAVEL

"All those who wander are not lost."
J. R. R. TOLKIEN

This simple line from Tolkien's Lord of The Rings speaks to me. I have spent my lifetime exploring every continent, getting lost occasionally, but finding myself along the way. I have learned that those who wander off the beaten track and rebel against the norms or status quo—we are not lost.

On the contrary, we are trailblazers pushing boundaries, discovering new possibilities, and mapping out pathways for future travelers. *Rebel Vegan Travel Guide* is committed to rethinking travel, by forging healthy and sustainable ways to get back out there in this brave new world.

REBEL VEGAN's mission neatly unites and brings together two of my great passions: veganism and travel. Both push you to think anew about the world and your place in it. Both will drive you out of your element and ask you to be a better version of yourself than you were when you woke up this morning.

Veganism and travel will ask you to rethink concepts you gave little thought to before, and to try things you've never considered trying. These lifestyles bring together and promote the values of community, sustainability, justice, and compassion.

Despite the bumps in the road, traveling as a vegan has been a huge blessing. It nudged me outside my safe places, pushed me to try new things, make deeper connections, get lost in the moments, and find myself along the way.

I'm living proof that traveling as a vegan is not only feasible, but also life affirming. It's only by going out and engaging with the world as your authentic self that you can thrive and get the most of any adventure. As an international guide leading people into unfamiliar places, I always aim to build strong bonds with my groups so they feel safe to fully open themselves up to new adventures, and to push themselves to the edges of their comfort zones. It's from this space that they can test themselves and the world, find out what they are made of, who they really are. Now I am asking the same of you on our journey together.

> *"The mind that opens up to a new idea never returns to its original size."*
> **ALBERT EINSTEIN**

THE NEW NORMAL: OUR BRAVE NEW WORLD

*"Even if I knew that tomorrow the world would go
to pieces, I would still plant my apple tree."*
MARTIN LUTHER KING JR.

This book has been a passion project and has helped steer me through some unknown and unexpected terrain. When Covid shut down the world, I was genuinely lost. For the first time, I was no longer living life as I knew it, having had a long life on the open road. Like most people, I hunkered down and hoped it would pass quickly.

As I looked out onto a world that was in chaos and fear, I knew I had to rally my pent-up energies and find a new purpose. If my travels have taught me anything, it's to think on your feet and move forward. That's when this travel guide was born, bringing together my two great passions: travel and veganism.

The ongoing pandemic has brought devastation and highlighted many uncomfortable truths. It has forced us all to stop and take stock, and to look anew at the world and our place in it. This hard-won fresh perspective has forever shifted how we live our lives and will inevitably alter how we travel and reconnect with the world.

Unwittingly, Covid highlighted the urgency of vegan values and is making us all more aware of the importance of living and traveling sustainably and ethically. As we emerge from our ongoing lockdowns, many of us are prioritizing our wellbeing, global health, and sustainability.

So while the Covid crisis may have derailed many of our holidays and put the brakes on foreign trips, in the end it is making vegan values and travel even more relevant. As the world rebounds from the effects of the pandemic, industries across the board are reinventing themselves—including the travel industry. Vegan-friendly tours, excursions, hotel suites, and travel apps are now emerging at exponential rates as more travelers demand a safer, kinder, and more respectful way to engage with the world.

One thing that hasn't changed is our primal impulse to explore and connect. It's integral to our quest to live life to the full and become the best versions of ourselves. This is why travel will always be important and we must rethink the old systems and draw up new maps to get us back out there in the world.

As you take these first steps back out into the world with these bold values at the forefront, my hope is that you will think of *Rebel Vegan Travel Guide* as a springboard to help you understand these connected and often complicated issues, along with being empowered to travel sustainably, and find a new way of connecting along the way.

Vegan travel is about compassion and sustainability. It's about being kinder to the planet, to the animals, to local communities, and to yourself.

"Oh, wonder! How many goodly creatures are there here!
How beauteous mankind is!
O brave new world, that has such people in it!"
WILLIAM SHAKESPEARE, THE TEMPEST

BEST FOOT FORWARD: TRAVELING WITH VEGAN VALUES

"The environment is where we all meet,
where all have a mutual interest.
It is the one thing all of us share."
LADY BIRD JOHNSON

Sustainable and ethical tourism has become a pillar for many travelers today. Covid has highlighted the need to change our behavior and has inadvertently advanced the vegan movement and its values to help solve many of the issues facing our world. After a couple years of restrictions and isolation, travel is at the top of many people's agenda.

According to the World Tourism Organization, sustainable travel refers to tourism that takes full account of its current and future economic, social, and environmental impacts while addressing the needs of visitors, the industry, the environment, and the host communities.[1]

This includes supporting the local economy, choosing the most eco-friendly form of transportation, boycotting irresponsible wildlife tourism companies, leaving a positive footprint, giving back to the community, and now, traveling vegan.

As a result, more and more people are choosing to incorporate veganism into travel plans as well as their daily lives. In the UK alone, the number of vegans has quadrupled during the last five years.[2] We are putting veganism on the map!

Sustainability and ethics are strong reasons to travel vegan, but they aren't the only reasons so many people are choosing to embrace a vegan lifestyle. At the core of veganism, we find many urgent issues and compelling reasons to incorporate this philosophy into every aspect of our lives. The mounting body of evidence is unequivocal: there are few things worse you can do for the health of humans, the planet and animals, for our air, water, Earth's atmosphere, than eat meat or consume animal products. *REBEL VEGAN* is your guide to taking these first steps back out into the world.

Whether it is a local staycation or a round-the-world adventure, we are intensely curious and social animals that need connection and to engage with our wider worlds. You are welcome at the *REBEL VEGAN* table regardless of why you are here or where you are going. This is a safe space to plan or pack for any plant-based adventure.

Inside this book, there are lots of inspiring stories and destinations for armchair travelers or those still in lockdowns. You are welcome whether your journey is still simply a vague idea that creeps up in those quiet moments before bed, or if you're a seasoned backpacker with a passport full of stamps.

If you picked up this guide because you are worried about finding other vegans while traipsing the globe, or because you refuse to spend another vacation living on peanuts and salad greens—you've come to the right place.

In this guide, I will provide you with the answers to your many questions about veganism and vegan travel. We will journey through both the past and the present, discussing the roots of veganism, as well as the impacts of the Covid pandemic on the way we are traveling as we begin to venture out once again. I will provide a welcoming, fully inclusive space to explore, contemplate, and decide what vegan travel means to you.

It's time to begin. We'll soon be surrounded by the colorful pagodas and columns adorned with dragons as we attend the Vegetarian Festival in Bangkok. Yellow flags and the sweet smell of Roti Sai Mai will fill the air. A turn of the page will take us to the city built on top of stilts: Amsterdam. Our night will be spent floating aboard a Woonark while gazing up at the starlit gothic buildings erected atop the city.

We'll awaken to the songs of tropical birds and the howls of monkeys in the jungle of Costa Rica. We can start our day off right with a satiating plate of Gallo Pinto and a refreshing glass of jugo sandía. In a blink of an eye, we will find ourselves in the hip and bustling city of Portland, Oregon. We'll shop 'til we drop at the world's first vegan mini-mall. (Maybe I'll even convince you to get a vegan-ink tattoo at Scapegoat.)

Together we will overcome any obstacles thrown our way. We will navigate both the cultural barriers and the exhilarating food markets. We will learn to ask for vegan plates in several languages and indulge in foreign delicacies with confidence. Most importantly, we make vegan travel easy, safe, and fun in this brave new world.

Buckle up and prepare for take-off.
Our adventure starts on the next page.

ACCIDENTAL VEGAN: MY VEGAN STORY

Every bump in the road while traveling brings new experiences to test yourself and grow. In hindsight, I feel grateful for coming down with severe Listeria[3], which caused me to become violently ill and seek refuge at a monastery outside of Hué, in northern Vietnam. After years working throughout South East Asia and eating street food, I thought I was invincible. Nothing seemed to get me down, and, until that point, I had never claimed a day's sickness in my working life.

After years of non-stop travel, I needed to find a safe oasis to shut down. This was extreme; I was burnt out at the end of the line. My initial instinct was to fly home, but I didn't think I could endure the long flight. Instead, I limped to one of my favorite places where I knew I would receive solitude and sanctuary. I needed to heal, and also to stay still and take stock of my life.

I had stopped at this monastery many times while leading tours through the mountains of northern Vietnam. It became a regular feature on my tours, and we became friends. But I never thought that one day, they would not only come to my rescue, but also change the course of my life.

The monks made a diagnosis and started their treatment. I was placed on a simple plant-based diet in conjunction with herbal remedies, without any discussion. I unwittingly became a vegan within the silent walls of this ancient religious community, and an accidental vegan activist was born. I may not have converted to Buddhism, but I became devoted to the values of veganism.

I believe we are all born vegan until we are corrupted and brainwashed by the dominant carnist belief system. So, in a way, I am a born again vegan!

After my recovery and rebirth, it was time to leave the safety of the monastery walls. But I was wholly ignorant of how to sustain my life on the road as a vegan. I didn't know the first thing about the basics of plant-based living. I had to ask how we could get milk without a lactating cow. Milk specially made for humans was a novel concept!

Instantly there were challenges and mishaps that I needed to navigate with diplomacy and caution. I also needed to educate and believe in myself. Luckily, I found a dog-eared old copy of Peter Singer's seminal classic: Animal Liberation: A New Ethics For Our Treatment of Animals. From these early challenges and research, *REBEL VEGAN LIFE* was born.

Immediately after waving goodbye to my monk saviors, I arrived in the empty, hot streets of a deserted Hué City. I hadn't been there with a group for many months, so I assumed I could quietly wander through the cluster of empty side streets. Then I heard a shriek, saw the flash of a vaguely familiar smiling face, before being propelled into the window table of a local restaurant.

The staff seemed to know me and were so enthusiastic that it seemed rude to fight it. Without a word, they went into the kitchen and brought me my favorite drink: a freshly sliced open coconut. Soon, the chef came out to welcome me back and, with elaborate gestures, presented me with what they remembered as my favorite dish on the menu: phở chín - beef noodle soup, a rare version of their classic Pho soup. They were genuinely ecstatic to see me, and it was a touching gesture to remember my usual orders after all this time. It was actually very humbling, as I recognized the disparity in our worlds. They seemed to remember every detail; I vaguely recalled bringing tour groups here. Although I had only been in the monastery for nine days, the meat-eater they remembered so well seemed unrecognizable to even me.

Their expectant eyes were on me, and my heart was racing. I knew I had to respect their kindness and protect their pride. So I grabbed my Vietnamese translator and told them about my recent discovery. While sharing this story, I stayed true to my newfound values and gained friends for life. Soon they had me in the kitchen explaining exactly what could be classed as vegan. Something seemed to click in the chef's mind, and he embraced the situation and challenge. Right in front of me, he made a version of my favorite phở brimming with all the colors of the garden. His pride was restored, and he christened it Todd's Special.

I have repeated this experience in various contexts and countries. Without exception, I have found colleagues and friends open to vegan values. It seems a natural fit to fit with their calm natures and Buddhist beliefs. I also found that they respond well to be included and respected. With this template, my connections grew stronger, and my world opened up. Many of those little roadside cafes grew to understand my choices and eventually started veganizing their menus to appeal to a new class of traveler.

When I return to these places, my friends still jump up and shriek, excited to show me their latest vegan creation. Todd's Special has become more standard, and my friends are proud to be part of this ongoing story. Slow but steady, we are veganizing the world. And now you are part of this story, part of the solution, a *REBEL VEGAN*.

1

HIDDEN HISTORIES
VEGANISM AROUND THE WORLD

"I have no doubt that it is a part of the destiny of the human race, in its gradual improvement, to leave off eating animals, as surely as the savage tribes have left off eating each other when they came in contact with the more civilized."
HENRY DAVID THOREAU

Before we begin our journey, let's first travel back in time to understand where and how it all began.

Before I land in any foreign place, I do my homework and learn their history. It is crucial in grasping each destination's customs and culture. And it forms the basis to understanding and connecting with the locals. In the end, after many years on the road, I have become a bit of a history geek.

Discovering your own hidden history can be hugely rewarding and invigorating. It is also transformative in understanding and appreciating who we are. Simply by making that direct link, you become part of the story and are strengthened with its sense of purpose. We are not the first to walk this path.

That's what is so empowering when you realize you are connected to others who came before you; they become our forefathers/mothers and a comforting source of ancestral power that you can draw on whenever you need a boost.

We are walking in their footsteps.

It is high time to reclaim our history and discover the roots of veganism around the world.

STANDING ON THE SHOULDERS OF GIANTS

Veganism has gotten a bad rap in recent years. It's been mistakenly bundled up with a long list of fad diets that have risen out of the blue, only to disappear in the blink of an eye. I'm sure you've heard about more than a few of these—some of the best-known examples are the Atkins and Keto diets.

Essentially, a fad diet[1] is a diet that becomes popular for a short time, similar to fads in fashion, without being a standard dietary recommendation, and often making unreasonable claims for fast weight loss or health improvements.

Neither veganism nor vegetarianism fits this description.

While many people think veganism sprang from the abyss and spread like wildfire these last several years, the reality is that the ideals of plant-based or ethical eating and compassion for other creatures took root in ancient times[2].

There are *REBEL VEGANS* throughout recorded history in every religious text. Their brave voices echo through the centuries. A few of our more noteworthy ancestors acting as a guiding light have been the Buddha, Pythagoras of Samos, St. Francis of Assisi, Leonardo da Vinci, Susan B. Anthony, Mary Shelley, and Benjamin Franklin.

These are the true trailblazers of vegan values. Without Lord Krishna preaching for the preparation of vegetables in his name, and without the poetry of William Blake urging us to think about the creation of all beings, where would veganism and animal rights activism be today?

These were the first Rebel Vegans to challenge and rethink the established belief systems of the day and go against the status quo[3]. They thought deeper about what they put on their plates and where it came from. The roots of ethical eating are made up of ancient Greek philosophers, Chinese Buddhist monks, an Egyptian Pharaoh, and even a North American colonialist. These larger-than-life characters challenged the dominant beliefs of their day, called out injustice in our cruel food systems, and are the original rebels.

As we embark on our vegan travels today, we stand proudly on their shoulders. So, with no further ado, let's meet these giants.

HISTORY OF VEGANISM

The Vegetarian Society was founded in 1847 in England. This society supported the movement away from the consumption of meat but had not delved deeper into the issue of animal exploitation at the time.

However, the original use of the word "vegetarian" doesn't match with how we use it today. When the word was first used in Britain in the 1830s, it was defined differently. A vegetarian at that time was a person who didn't eat any animal products, and also extended that non-use of animals to clothing. The meaning of vegetarian was actually very close to our current definition of "vegan."[4]

Leslie Cross sparked a change when the society's magazine, The Vegetarian Messenger, published a letter he wrote denouncing the use of cow's milk. Society members went wild with debate. Was this the next step for those on the vegetarian path, or was this going too far?

When the society refused to add a non-dairy faction to their newsletter after a lengthy petition, Donald Watson, a friend of Cross and secretary of the Leicester, England branch, solicited all vegetarians who had an interest in explicitly rejecting all non-human exploitation to join him in a new venture. With fifty responses to his ad, he went on to form the Vegan Society in November 1944. The original group consisted of just twenty-five members.[5]

A die-hard vegan until death, Watson predicted that at his funeral there would be "a smattering of people, but there'll be the spirits of all the animals I've never eaten. In that case, it'll be a big funeral." He passed away at 95, and I'd like to think that his funeral was a regular barnyard party.

Watson chose the word "vegan" because he believed it signified the beginning and end of "vegetarian." In 1949, friend and colleague Cross realized the need for one consistent definition of veganism. In 1951, he finally laid out a concrete definition and ruleset based on suggestions from readers in his articles "The New Constitution" and "Veganism Defined."

The society may not have written a solid definition of veganism until 1951, yet the practice of avoiding the consumption of animal meat can be traced back more than 2,500 years to ancient Indian and Eastern Mediterranean societies. Although the word didn't exist then, vegans and vegetarians certainly did.

The first mention of vegetarianism was by the Greek philosopher and mathematician, Pythagoras of Samos, around 500 BCE. Along with many other academic concepts, he promoted benevolence among all species, including humans.

Pythagoras advocated the idea that all animals had immortal souls which would be reincarnated after death. He believed so strongly in the good a cruelty-free diet could create that he had his students live on a raw-vegan diet for 40 days before entering his school. In fact, until the word vegetarianism was birthed over 2,000 years later in 1815, people who avoided meat were called Pythagoreans.

> *"As long as man continues to be the ruthless destroyer of lower living beings he will never know health or peace. For as long as men massacre animals, they will kill each other."*
> **PYTHAGORAS[6]**

It was around this same time that Siddhartha Gautama, or Buddha, was sharing the idea of vegetarian diets with his followers. Many religions, including Buddhism, Jainism, Hinduism, and Taoism, encourage and even mandate plant-based diets.[7]

This is largely due to their adhesion to ahimsa (non-violence), karma (ill-effects on oneself as a consequence of ill-treatment of others), reincarnation (rebirth of a passed soul into a new body), and a general reverence for nature and all of its creatures.

Even the Torah and minority groups of the Christian faith advocate adhering to a cruelty-free diet in order to attain religious redemption.

COUNTRIES WITH A HISTORY OF VEGANISM[8]

INDIA[9]

In Indian culture, the practice of non-violence, or ahimsa, has informed meat-free living. India has been known for its vegetarianism since ancient times, with scriptures such as the Rig Veda and the Bhagavad Gita preaching compassion for our animal companions. These scriptures are believed to have been written as long ago as 400-250 BCE.

> *"Meat can never be obtained without injury to living creatures, and injury to sentient beings is detrimental to the attainment of heavenly bliss; let him therefore shun the use of meat. Having well considered the disgusting origin of flesh and the cruelty of fettering and slaying corporeal beings, let him entirely abstain from eating flesh."*
> **RIG-VEDA (10.87.16)**

Unfortunately, cultural values in India are rapidly changing, and eating flesh is beginning to be increasingly socially acceptable. New restaurants serving fast food and western cuisines are tempting Indians to try meat-based dishes, and many are falling prey. Even so, there are still approximately 360 million vegetarian people in India—about 20% of the population.

CHINA[10]

Vegetarianism has been an integral part of the Chinese diet since its ancient beginnings. According to legend, the first prophet, Fu Xi, was vegetarian and taught people to settle down and plant seeds. The next prophets taught people to make medicines from herbs and clothes from cotton. The ancients' way of life was based on compassion, inner-spiritualism, naturalism, pacifism, and vegetarianism.

It's estimated that today approximately 50 million Chinese people follow a vegetarian diet. The entanglement with vegetarianism and veganism in China stems from their religious beliefs, mainly Buddhism and Taoism.

Approximately half the world's Buddhists live in China, and they account for about eighteen percent of the country's total population. Another ten percent of the population practices Taoism. These religions tend to follow strict vegetarian diets and frequently exclude eggs and dairy. Influenced by these compassion-based diets, plant-based foods like tofu and mock-meat have become an integral part of the national cuisine.

GREECE[11]

Vegetarianism had its first famous debut in Greece, where the philosopher Pythagoras preached the righteousness of a vegan diet. He claimed that eating animals was unhealthy and caused humans to wage war on one another.

He recognized that animal agriculture industry was a system of normalized violence, leading to widespread complacency and acceptance of otherwise gruesome acts. He wasn't the only Greek philosopher planting these seeds.

Plato had once written in The Republic that "the ideal city was a vegetarian city" on the grounds that meat was a luxury, leading to decadence and war. As early as 270 CE comes one of the first records of a vegetarian diet. Classic philosopher Plotinus wrote about how humans must treat all animals with compassion.

In more recent years, meat—excluding fish, which is widely consumed in Greece—continues to be considered a luxury item due to the prohibitive cost of raising animals for food. Fruit, vegetables, and other nutritious foods make up the bulk of the traditional Greek diet. This diet is commonly referred to as the Mediterranean Diet, which is revered as one of the healthiest diets in the world.

JAMAICA[12]

The tropical climate and religious culture of Jamaica have led to a vegan-friendly national cuisine. Jamaica is home to the Rastafari religion, of which many followers have adopted a diet named Ital, derived from the word vital. This diet is based on local, organic foods, and for many Rastas is interpreted as being entirely vegetarian or vegan. This is based on the belief that eating dead meat would run counter to their Livity elevation, meaning the life force conferred by the Almighty Jah (God), which they believe exists within all living beings.

Rastafarians also believe that people are naturally vegetarian based on human physiology and anatomy, a belief increasingly held by archeologists and biologists.

Many Jamaicans have developed their own versions of a vegan one-pot stew dressed with coconut milk and designed to strengthen their connection to nature.

JAPAN[13]

The Japanese avoided eating meat for more than 12 centuries. In fact, the consumption of meat was banned in the 6th century when Buddhism was brought over from neighboring Korea. According to the Moral Precepts, the killing of animals was morally prohibited, and meat was classified as a bodily toxin. Punishment for consuming meat included fasting, repenting, and even temporary suspension from their shrine.

Depending on the animal consumed, this punishment could last anywhere from five to one hundred and fifty days. All of this led to the staple diet of the Buddhist monks, Shojin Ryorin, which is vegan by default. The only exceptions to this rule were the occasional aristocratic hunt and doctor-prescribed medicinal meat products.

Dietary practices began to change when Emperor Meiji came into power in 1868. In an attempt to fast-track assimilation to Western practices and technologies, he began to denounce the cultural meat taboos. The emperor emphasized this to the public by eating beef on the day of the New Year in 1872, causing a group of Buddhist monks to raid the Imperial Palace, claiming that the new trend of eating meat was "destroying the soul of the Japanese People."

Japanese cuisine has quickly given way to meat-based dishes from Korea, China, and especially the West. According to the Japanese Tourism Agency, only around 4% of Japan is vegetarian today. The national cuisine of Japan includes a significant amount of seafood and fish, especially in archipelagos such as Okinawa. Even so, plant-based foods still remain an integral part of the country's diet, including staple items such as tofu and fermented soybeans.

ISRAEL[14]

Israel, and in particular Judaism, has a long past of compassion for animals. The principle of tza'ar ba'alei chayim (the suffering of living creatures) prohibits unnecessary suffering to animals. Judaism's adherence to a Kosher diet is in no way the most humane choice they could have made, though it has primed the population to think about what they eat. In addition to this, many traditional Israeli dishes include vegetables, fruits, and grains. Dishes including couscous, hummus, falafel, baba ganoush, and dolma are all often accidentally vegan.

In recent years, Israel has been named the world's leading vegan destination. It also ranks top of the world with five percent of its population identifying as vegan. And, with over 400 restaurants, Tel-Aviv is considered one of the most vegan-friendly cities on the planet. This number has more than doubled since 2010 and shows the world what is possible.

PLANT-BASED LIFESTYLES MOVE WEST[15]

North America saw its first big news flash about the strange new world of vegetarianism with the start of a religious sect in Pennsylvania—although it went terribly wrong in this scenario. This sect is an example of a restrictive lifestyle, countering the view of veganism I support, which enables the individual to open up their world.

The Ephrata Cloister opened its doors in 1732, inviting followers to join in their watch for the coming of Christ. Members slept on wooden benches for six hours a night and were given one small vegetarian meal a day. The rigorously restrictive religious community died out quickly.[16]

Following this, vegetarianism was more positively introduced to the public by English philosopher and social reformer Jeremy Bentham. Bentham preached that human superiority was as equally unjust as racism, stating that animal suffering was just as serious as human suffering. He gifted us one of my favorite quotes and words to live by:

"The question is not, can they reason, nor can they talk, but, can they suffer?"

This quote is still pertinent today as veganism quickly moves into the grounds of the social justice movement.

By the year 1850, the American Vegetarian Society had gotten its start. This was just three years after the Vegetarian Society was formed in England. On the other hand, while Donald Watson founded the first vegan society in England in 1844, it took the United States a long and painful 104 years to catch up with a vegan society of their own. We can thank Catherine Nimmo and Rubin Abramowitz for finally getting the society up and running.

Veganism gained another boost in the west in 1960, when twenty-six-year-old H. Jay Dinshah founded a second vegan society - the American Vegan Society. He was the first person in the west to link veganism to the Sanskrit concept of ahimsa or non-violence.

Merely two years later, the word 'Vegan' was published by the Oxford Illustrated Dictionary. The first published definition of the word was basic and somewhat lacking. It defined a vegan as: "A vegetarian who eats no butter, eggs, cheese, or milk".

And then, the idea really took off. During the 1960s and 70s, the vegetarian lifestyle became a centric value of the counterculture that was thriving across the United States due to the controversial Vietnam War. The counterculture encouraged people to think about both their diets and the environment, instilling a sense of distrust of the current food production systems and the corporations behind them.

In the following decades, research emerged that clearly pointed to the idea that diets based on animal fats and proteins are malicious to our health. In addition to this, two major North American dietitians' associations, the American Dietetic Association and the Dietitians of Canada came forward in 2003 telling us that vegan diets are in fact suitable and healthy for all life stages[17]. The British Dietetic Association released a similar statement in 2014[18].

DEVELOPMENT OF THE MODERN DIET[19]

The foundation of our modern diet traces back ten thousand years to the first agricultural revolution when animals were first forced into the hopeless life of domestication for slaughter. This sounds like a long time, yet in evolutionary terms it is a quick blink of the eye,

Before we built factories to produce our food, and before we paid farmers to work the fields, we ate from the Earth. Early humans were mostly hunters and gatherers. Studies have found that early-age humans who adhered to food in its raw, natural form didn't suffer from the common diseases of our time, such as high blood pressure, atherosclerosis, and cardiovascular disease.

When the agricultural revolution struck, more and more land was being taken away from the nomadic hunter-gatherer tribes for farming. These groups of people were pushed into the corners of the planet, where their numbers have naturally diminished. Today, there are only a handful of tribes still living on a stone-age diet. As such, the modified meat-heavy diet of the day paired with our new sedentary lifestyle has led to an abundance of health issues. And while seventy-three percent of modern-day hunter-gatherer tribes consume more than half of their calories in meat, it is believed that most tribes derived seventy percent of their caloric intake from plant-based sources, in addition to increments of time when their diets consisted of only a handful or so of meat a week[20].

It is accepted that humans have a complicated connection and history of meat eating. But can we adapt to be healthy herbivores? Some scientists argue that eating meat was a key factor in human evolution by allowing the early Homo Erectus to grow a larger brain than its ape companions, while other scientists highlight that our prehistoric ancestors started off on a plant-based diet because you can't tear flesh by hand or tear hide without larger canines.

Regardless of where we started, Geneticist Sarah Tishkoff of the University of Pennsylvania sidesteps the whole debate and calls it irrelevant. They have proven that our DNA has changed since then. We aren't the same humans as we once were. If our genetic makeup has evolved, why not our diets too?

NOT NATURAL BORN KILLERS:
FIVE REASONS WHY HUMANS AREN'T DESIGNED TO EAT MEAT:

- We don't like blood. 99.9% of humans cannot stand the sight of blood and intestines, nor the sounds of an animal dying. Most of us can't stomach the bloody reality of eating an animal.

- We lack the physical tools. Real carnivores have large canine teeth and sharp claws that can tear flesh from prey. Humans have small, dull canines and short soft fingernails. Humans also have flat molars like herbivores, to grind plant foods like fruit and vegetables.

- Our digestive systems can't take it. Carnivores have short digestive tracts that allow the meat to pass quickly through their system. The human digestive tract is much longer, which gives the fiber and nutrients in plant foods enough time to be broken down and absorbed.

- We don't have the right stomach acid. Carnivores have strong stomach acid that can break down raw meat and kill any bacteria present. Human stomach acid is similar to plant-eating animals. It is strong, but not strong enough to kill some bacteria found in meat. This is why we must cook meat to eat it. But cooking meat at high temperatures creates substances (heterocyclic amines and polycyclic aromatic hydrocarbons) that cause DNA mutations and increase the risk of cancer.

- Meat makes us sick. According to the American Heart Association, meat-eaters have a 32% higher risk of developing heart disease than vegetarians. If we are meant to eat meat, then why is it killing us?

VEGANISM IN TODAY'S WORLD[21]

"Nothing is more powerful than an idea whose time has come."
VICTOR HUGO[22]

We now know that the practice of plant-based eating has been around since ancient times. However, these ideals have mostly been tucked away in monasteries and other religious sects for most of history. In 2010, this changed. Veganism went mainstream[23].

Why now? Experts hypothesize that an increase in the use of social media has led to more awareness of the ethical and sustainability issues surrounding meat. Also, it has simply become easier to be a vegan with mock-meat and non-dairy cheese available at most popular grocers. And it's about time.

This is the time when people of all groups of humanity are working to reclaim their history. As a society, we are rethinking and sharing the truth of history. Women, minority racial sects, LGBTQ+, animals, and vegans are reclaiming our histories - and with them our rights.

In 2010, the European Parliament defined the meaning of vegan for food labels. This regulation went active by 2015. Chain restaurants took notice of this underserved market and began clearly denoting vegan items on their menus. Supermarkets also stepped up by improving their selection of vegan processed foods, many dedicating entire sections of the store to vegan products[24].

Veganism is still misunderstood in many parts of the world. Yet as a traveler, it's never been easier to connect with fellow vegans. Being part of this movement provides us with a ready-made community in all sects of the world, ready to help us thrive during our expeditions abroad.

CURRENT AFFAIRS[25]

According to the International Food Information Council, more people are moving to plant-based protein during the COVID-19 pandemic. Meat shortages and a desire for greater overall health have piqued interest in plant-derived meals. While a number of everyday items became scarce on our grocer's shelves, and our local eateries closed their doors for now, and some even for good, we have begun to think about what, where, when, and how we eat in a different way than we've had to do before.

The interest in adopting a vegan lifestyle continues to develop as news leaks out about unjust employee treatment at meatpacking plants and inhumane treatment of animals at meat farms. The headlines warning about environmental catastrophe looming in the not-so-distant future due partially to how we produce and consume our food increases the urgency and importance of veganism.

WHY THE INCREASED INTEREST?

Let's back up a second. Did you catch the part where I said COVID-19 is influencing people to go vegan? It seems unrelated at first, doesn't it? Yet according to Proagrica, 18% of Brits have eaten more vegetarian and vegan food items since the start of the pandemic in March 2020, and at least one-fifth of those people plan to continue with this new lifestyle. What's the catch?

There are many theories as to why this is the case, one being that people are beginning to feel that plant-based alternatives to meat are healthier and easier to access in these times. Another theory focuses on the quarantine aspect of the pandemic. Many people are trying to use quarantine as a way to get healthier and improve their nutrition.

People are also seeing nature thrive as humans step away momentarily, taking their pollution with them. These things aren't going unnoticed, and they're inciting change.

The most pressing theory is the association between factory farming and deadly diseases. We may never know conclusively how Covid started but the conditions of the wet markets in China and our own factory farms in our backyards are the ideal breeding grounds for this type of pathogen to spread from non-human to human animals. Then in today's globally connected world, that virus will take hold around the world and become another international health crisis waiting to happen.

An estimated 60% of all viruses that infect humans come from animals, and 75% of new infectious diseases are zoonotic (caused by germs that spread between animals and people). Most zoonotic diseases arise because of the conditions the animals are kept in. Wet markets[26] are prime examples, where we've seen the rise of outbreaks of avian influenza and diseases like SARS[27].

Modern animal processing houses their stock (living animals) in extremely cramped conditions ideal for spreading disease. In this way, viruses like Covid are largely intertwined with the maltreatment of animals worldwide. Sadly, this fact leads to even further maltreatment. Often entire flocks or herds are slaughtered in an attempt to control the spread of viruses and diseases. Many times, this is done in vain, as once transmission is made from animal to human to human, containment is impossible in the modern globalized world.

There is a history of zoonosis. thanks to the practice of humans eating their animal companions. Some viruses that have affected the human race which are thought to have stemmed from animals include HIV from the butchering of a nonhuman primate for human consumption, and Creutzfeldt-Jakob disease, better known as Mad Cow Disease.

Mad Cow Disease resulted from humans eating meat from cows, but not just any cows. These poor animals had been fed meat by-products from other cows, and it was this eating of its own species that brought about Mad Cow disease, to both the cows and the people who ate them.

Worryingly, it is far more common for humans to respond to pandemics than to act to prevent them. However, this may be starting to change. People are realizing the impact farming conditions and animal consumption have on global and public health. People are learning that real prevention requires taking steps to minimize the chance of a virus emerging in the first place. Finally, and thankfully, they are beginning to appraise how animals are treated and are taking issue with the inhumane practices they are subjected to[28].

There is still much to learn and many challenges to face. However, it is clear that veganism is more than a passing fad diet or the latest trending hashtag. The values that veganism espouses are an integral part of solving many of the issues facing our world today, from world hunger, and the climate crisis, to stopping future pandemics.

By retracing our history, we recognize that our earliest ancestors evolved on a mainly plant-based diet, both from necessity and limited hunting ability. Ethical eating and compassion for animals have been part of our earliest religions and philosophies. And for the last seven decades, veganism has become a well-defined and strong movement, spurred on not only by animal welfare, but also due to the fact that our current meat-centric diets and food systems threaten our very existence.

By embracing your history, you can feel secure in your choices and confident that you are part of a movement fighting for justice and compassion around the world.

VEGAN STATISTICS[29]

Our first journey together has been a success. We now know where veganism comes from, and how it has developed over the years. We have seen examples of communities thriving on plant-based diets, from the ancient Buddhist monks to the modern-day beach bums of Costa Rica. We're almost ready to join them by creating our own vegan adventures and memories. First, I'd like to quickly get you up to speed on some of the latest vegan statistics.

- Vegan diets are linked to a thirty-five percent reduced risk of prostate cancer. Forty-five percent of the Earth's land is used for farming livestock in some way.

- As of 2020, the size of the global vegan food market is calculated to be worth $17 billion.

- Plant-based meat covers two percent of all packaged meat options.

- More than thirty-nine percent of people in the United States are adding more vegan food options to the dishes they eat.

- Europe represents thirty-nine percent of the global market for meat alternatives.

- It's expected that the market for vegan meat alternatives will hit $7.5 billion globally by 2025.

- If the world went vegan, it would save 8-million human lives by 2050, reduce greenhouse gas emissions from agriculture by two-thirds, and lead to healthcare-related savings and avoided climate damages of $1.5 trillion.

- Worldwide, more than 70 billion land animals are killed for food every year.

- Since 1970, the collective weight of free-living animals has declined eighty-two percent, leaving a controlled number of farmed animals to dominate the global biomass.

- By going vegan for one month, you would save thirty animal lives, 620 pounds of harmful carbon dioxide emissions, 913 square feet of forest, and 33,481 gallons of water.

2

A CAUTIONARY TALE
POST-COVID TRAVEL[1]

"All great changes are preceded by chaos."
DEEPAK CHOPRA[2]

When I decided on the title of this chapter, I believed that we were on the cusp of living in a post-Covid world. I still believe that—we are our way. The problem is that we are not actually LIVING in a post-Covid world. The road has more bumps and the journey longer than any of us could have envisioned.

We thought we had it beat when the vaccines were developed. Most of the world breathed a sigh of relief as COVID-19 vaccinations were made available and administered. But that sense of safety didn't last long.

Even after vaccinations for COVID-19 were made available in many countries, in late 2020 a mutation called Delta brought new fears. This Delta version quickly became the predominant SARS CoV-2 variant in the U.S. and the U.K. And again, we're comforted, knowing that our current vaccinations afford protection against Delta too.

But now we're facing a new peril, a mutation named Omicron. As I write this at the start of a new year, 2022, the news claims are alarming. This new version is so contagious that within two weeks of its identification in South Africa, it was responsible for the majority of the Covid cases in that country.

In spite of all these ongoing challenges and fears, travel is still happening. People are still getting on planes, eating in restaurants, taking trains, and driving cars to new destinations.

We are all suffering from Covid fatigue and missing the freedoms of our old lives. Although I am grateful for my health, the past couple years of staying put has been personally challenging for me. Before the pandemic, I had spent II years traveling across the globe, guiding others in their own travel adventures. So after almost two years of isolation in London, I'm aching for all the fresh experiences and new people that only travel brings my way. I've set March 2022 as my target date to return to southeast Asia, one of my favorite places in the world.

However, if the dangers of these new variants linger and prevent my travel, I'll need to rethink my plans. We need to be extra agile in these uncertain times. Maybe I will refocus my need for adventure and go off on a solo trip around Scotland and sleep in a minivan. That's what the Staycation chapter is all about—discovering the beauty that's always been around you while staying local and safe. At times like these, it is sometimes the smartest and kindest thing to do.

With international travel we must remain vigilant and do the right thing. My advice is stay informed but not to let fear get the best of you. We must protect each other by educating ourselves and being aware of what is waiting for us in the countries we travel to—and be mindful of more than Covid. We must be aware of any type of threat in our travels.

But being up-to-date of the status of Covid in your destination country is imperative. That status can change quickly so in the days before you depart, check for Covid updates.

> *"One's destination is never a place,*
> *but a new way of seeing things."*
> **HENRY MILLER**[3]

The Covid pandemic has caused widespread change on both global and personal levels. It has brought the world together and caused all of us to gain a newfound respect for each other, animals, and the environment. It's placed what we eat and our health at the forefront of our minds. It has taught us to re-engage and connect in a more sustainable and compassionate way. And most importantly, it has shown us what's possible when we all band together for a cause.

It's been a time of uncertainty and fear, a time of loss intertwined with a time of the overwhelmingly new—new concepts, new regulations, new ways to mourn, to celebrate, to live, to think, to travel, to connect, and even simply to be.

It's a mouthful to even say all the changes that have unraveled from this event, and far more than that to endure them as a humble human being. No industry, cause, family, or person has gone untouched by this trying time, me included.

EVERYONE HAS A COVID STORY - HERE'S MINE:

We have all lived through our generation's defining epoch; when everything changes, and we are thrust into a new era. There were our lives pre and, now, post-Covid. My pre-Covid life was like a kaleidoscope of exotic places, people, colors, and flavors. I reveled in spreading vegan values and seeing how healthy and ethical eating can change lives.

When COVID hit and borders came crashing down, this all came screeching to a halt. Before I could fully grasp how serious this would become, my company doors were closing. Life as I knew it had dissipated right before my eyes. After years of constant travel, I knew I needed to stop and take stock.

I couldn't see it at the time, but COVID was pushing, no, propelling me into the next chapter of my life. My time on the road was a fantastic adventure, but the travel gods had decided it was time to reset.

So I dusted myself off and took advantage of the enforced isolation. Within the quiet stillness of that strange time, I recognized that I had something unique to share and refocused my passion from curating vegan adventures towards supporting new ways to travel and live in a post-pandemic world. *Rebel Vegan Travel Guide* was born out of these tumultuous times and created to help navigate our way out and build a better, more sustainable future for travel.

The loveliest part of all of this is that now instead of inspiring a small number of people to experience veganism and travel, I have the opportunity to support far more people in finding their feet and understanding travel in these uncertain times.

When one door closes, another opens. From the upheavals of COVID, I believe we can see the world through a new lens and create a better way to live, work, and travel.

A NEW PERSPECTIVE FOR A NEW ERA:

"It was the best of times, it was the worst of times, it was the age of wisdom, it was the age of foolishness, it was the epoch of belief, it was the epoch of incredulity, it was the season of light, it was the season of darkness, it was the spring of hope, it was the winter of despair."
CHARLES DICKENS, A TALE OF TWO CITIES

Understandably, we tend to focus on the negative aspects of the pandemic. Bad news and fear sells papers, and is great clickbait. Yet during this time, people have been noticing the absurdities in our modern-day society, and the huge impact on certain racial and species groups.

As we recover from Covid and build new ways of doing things, our new normal, there is an increased consciousness and the starting of a movement. A respect for the environment and the future of the planet has grown. Our health is finally at the forefront of our attention. And at last, our relationship and treatment of animals, wild and farmed, has been highlighted and shown to be pivotal for all of our futures.

The world became smaller as we watched country after country, and continent after continent, fall prey to this virus. Our empathy has grown as we watched others suffer through the same traumas and overcome the same difficulties as our own. There has been division, but there has also been a notion of us against Covid—for once the 'us' being the global population.

I'm sure many of you have a similar Covid story to mine. Jobs, loved ones, and favorite pastimes that were taken away from us. We have all needed to adapt, rethink, and reinvent our lives.

But this is when we find out what we are made of and start to live our best lives. It's time to pick up the pieces, dust ourselves off, and reset. It's time to come out of this pandemic and into the new world to start our next chapter.

This time around, we have the opportunity to take our time and really connect with a place and its people, to treasure those random encounters, start new friendships, and understand who we are.[4]

THE TOURISM INDUSTRY AFTER COVID

"There is no education like adversity."
DISRAELI

In 2019, the tourism industry contributed over ten percent to the GDP (Gross Domestic Product) worldwide. That works out to around $2,890 billion, to help give you an understanding of how large of a contribution ten percent is. Covid shutdowns dropped this number to virtually zero overnight[5], hurting geographic regions that depend on tourism to keep their economies afloat. Economies of many regions have grown to rely heavily on tourism, and were hit particularly hard when Covid shut down travel, decimating the industry.

For instance, the sudden drop in tourism cost Venice more than one billion euros in lost revenues. While this was no doubt hard on Venice, it can be downright devastating for underdeveloped regions who don't have the resources to wait for the next wave of tourists.

According to a UNWTO survey, the industry's recovery will be slow, with only a third of the usual visitors turning out for the high season of 2021[6]. We have all missed our adventures.

However, this slow period has resulted in a number of positive changes. The crises have created an opportunity for future travel to be more sustainable by developing economies that can continue to involve tourism, while also having a basis in other economic areas.

In addition to this, the travel industry has also shifted their focus to inclusivity. Specialized travel agencies and tour companies are working to fill the underserved niche communities, considering things such as race, gender, identity, disabilities, diet requirements, ethics, and more.

Another positive that has come from this slow period is a focus on responsible and eco-friendly travel. We've yet to see what the industry is to decide on in this area, but talk of fly-free days, green-hotels, and movement away from animal exploitation are finally on the agenda.

*"A journey of a thousand miles
starts with a single step."*
LAO TZU

REBEL VEGAN'S NEW AGENDA:
SPENDING LOCAL/PREVENTING LEAKAGE[7]

*"Once in a while it really hits people
that they don't have to experience the world
in the way they have been told to."*
ALAN KEIGHTLEY

Tourism isn't the only thing being updated post-Covid. Travelers' ideals and priorities are being adapted as well. In the past, most of the travel industry has been focused on the mass tourism space, which is characterized by generic experiences, revenue leakage to international corporations, and environmental issues. Our new and improved focus and itineraries consist of supporting local businesses, protecting the environment, and fostering respect and empathy for all people and places.

We mentioned earlier that billions of dollars are being deposited into the global GDP annually by the travel industry, which on the surface seems like a good thing. The problem is that most of this money never reaches the local economy. It's been determined that less than ten percent of revenue actually makes it into the pockets of local business owners.

Where does this money go? Many of the travel expenses incurred in preparation for a trip—such as airfare, insurance, and travel agency fees—go to international companies with no relation to the region you are visiting.

This holds true for hotel stays at international chains or stays reserved externally through international booking websites as well. Even some excursions, experiences, and culture-based classes are managed by external companies who have nothing to do with the locale.

In this brave new world, more and more travelers are being mindful to shop, fly, and sleep locally to ensure their spending benefits the community they are experiencing, and not another faceless corporation.

I strongly recommend seeking out and trying these local gems yourself, reader. It not only helps the community, but it is always a far richer experience to engage with the local community and see exactly who your money is helping.

REBEL VEGAN'S NEW AGENDA:
PREVENTING POLLUTION

*"How is it possible that the most intellectual
creature to ever walk the planet earth
is destroying its only home?"*
JANE GOODALL[8]

Covid provided an opportunity for people to recognize the carbon footprint that travel can involve, leading them to rethink why and how they travel.

Travelers are demanding responsible travel policies be put in place. A report by Booking.com tells us that 53% of global travelers want to "travel more sustainably in the future, as Coronavirus has opened their eyes to humans' impact on the environment." [9]

Luckily, the industry is listening. The airlines have used the slowing of operations to update their fleets. Two major airlines in the UK will be rolling out a long-haul fleet that emits half the CO_2 than the fleet they operated pre-pandemic. United Airlines followed suit by ordering fifteen net-zero carbon supersonic aircraft for their fleet[10]. Hotels can now be certified "green," and on the planning end of the industry, a number of travel advisors are now specializing in eco-friendly tourism.

Travelers can help prevent travel-related pollution by doing things differently. The trend is shifting and many of us are now seek quality over quantity, meaning longer, less frequent trips.

It's finally understood that it is less important to check off as many places as quickly as possible, and more important to enjoy the opportunity to immerse yourself in the places that you visit. Slow, mindful travel—overland when possible—is the way to go.

REBEL VEGAN TOP TIP:

Check the website Book Different before choosing your accommodation to see how they rank in terms of eco-friendliness.

https://www.bookdifferent.com/en/

REBEL VEGAN'S NEW AGENDA:
ENDING OVER-TOURISM

"Difficult roads lead to beautiful destinations."
REBEL VEGAN

In the old version of tourism, many cities became tourism monocultures. We touched on this idea when explaining how leakage happens. The same hotels, experiences, and big-box companies move in to take hold of the profits at hand. As these cities become must-see destinations, and then fall prey to the consequences of mass tourism.

Destinations suffering from mass tourism become overwhelmed by tourists. Increases in rent, overcrowding of public spaces, pressure on local transportation systems, inflation rises in goods and services, intensive pollution, natural landscape damage, and shortage of housing for locals due to companies buying up homes to turn into vacation rentals, are some of the negative consequences that the communities we visit must manage and absorb.

To avoid contributing to the negative effects of mass tourism, take the road less traveled. Visit the lesser-known communities.

These destinations will be cheaper, less crowded, more authentic, and likely more tolerant of foreigners. Often, the off-the-beaten-path locations are where the intrepid traveler earns their richest travel stories.

But don't despair if you are dying to go to a highly publicized destination, you can mitigate many of the negatives by being mindful to spend your money in the local economy, staying in a family-run hotel, or heading there during the off-season. Simply by seeking out and eating at a local vegan cafe, you are being the change you want to see in the world.

Overall, the world of travel is far from perfect. Like anything else, it has an impact on the world, both negative and positive. What I hope you take away from this chapter is the opportunity to demand change through action. You have the power to make a difference through sustainable vegan travel.

That's the *REBEL VEGAN* way!

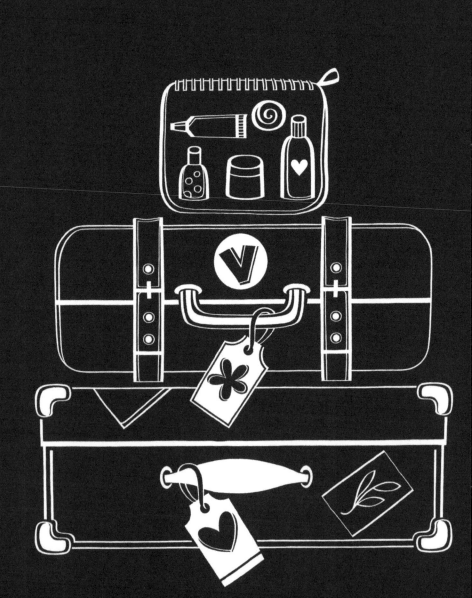

3

PLANNING & PACKING
TAKING VEGANISM ON THE ROAD

"A goal without a plan is just a wish."
ANTOINE DE SAINT-EXUPÉRY[1]

Failure to plan is to plan to fail. This is the motto I use when on the road. While it is important to be flexible, it is imperative to be prepared. The questions I like to focus on are: "What do we need to bring?," "What will we eat?," and "Will we cook in or eat out?" The answers to these three questions can inform many of your travel decisions such as where your holiday should take place, what type of accommodation you book, and what sort of budget is needed.

These questions can be daunting for any traveler, not to mention one who needs to consider a lifestyle rooted in animal compassion and plant-based foods. Foreign places can seem overwhelming with their unfamiliar customs, cuisines, and ways of thinking. But with a little planning and armed with our *REBEL VEGAN* resources, it can be a piece of vegan cake.

In this chapter, we will consider and weight up the options for your perfect plant-based adventure. We will walk through the preparations and explore what resources are out there to help us. We'll even write out a basic packing list that you can print out and use for any adventure—whether its a weekend away or a trip around the world.

WHAT TO RESEARCH BEFORE SETTING OFF

"Research is formalized curiosity.
It is poking and prying with a purpose."
- ZORA NEALE HURSTON[2]

Finding the right accommodation, ensuring proper nutrition, being prepared to acclimate to local culture and customs, and knowing what will make this journey rewarding and exciting for you are the most important things to keep in mind when planning your *REBEL VEGAN* travel adventure.

To decide what kind of accommodation you should book, consider whether or not you need a kitchen and how much privacy you prefer.

Are you an extrovert who likes to be around other people, and want to cook your own meals? Book a dorm bed in a hostel with a shared kitchen available for guest use.

Do you want a quiet vacation where meals are prepared for you? A bed and breakfast where you have your own quarters but can head to the dining room at mealtimes might be your ideal spot.

Personally, I fall in the middle. I like to stay at an accommodation with a shared kitchen where I can meet other people traveling the region. However, I almost always opt for a private bedroom.

Before heading to your destination of choice, look into the local cuisine. Find out if the veggies are traditionally sauteed in butter, or if the rice is usually cooked in beef broth. This way, you know how to double-check with your waiter or host family that your plate is safe to eat. Learn how to explain your dietary needs in the local language, or have them printed out on note cards. Check out the resource section at the back of this book for apps and websites that can help you do this.

It can be helpful to research the local grocery stores and natural food markets before arriving as well. Check out what local fruits, veggies, and plant-based snacks will be available. This can save you the trouble of running from place to place looking for your favorite items, and might even inspire you to try something new. If you plan on eating out, you can pre-find vegan restaurants along with their reviews and ratings on HappyCow (a vegetarian/vegan food directory), Yelp, or TripAdvisor.

Look up the average cost of living in the area you are visiting to get an idea of how much you will need to spend on groceries and meals out. Always come prepared to spend more money than you anticipate as the vegan items you are used to having in your diet such as soy milk, protein alternatives, vitamins, and other supplements might not be as easy to find in other countries. Bear in mind that when you do find these items it's possible they will be more expensive than they are back home.

Bring what you really need, and find what you can. As for the rest, be flexible. Try new products and focus on getting what you need nutritionally from the local produce. The previous book in this series, *REBEL VEGAN LIFE: A Plant-based Nutrition & Beginner's Guide*, lists all of the vitamins, minerals, and gut bacteria you need to thrive, as well as what natural vegan foods provide them. Throw this nutritional guide in your suitcase to make supplementing easy on the go.

TO COOK OR NOT TO COOK?

The answer to this question can define your travel experience, and having done your homework before you leave, will eliminate stress and save you time while you are abroad. Having a plan can even help you stick to your budget, allowing you to travel even further. Things to consider include:

- **Budget:** Food can easily become the most expensive part of your trip, especially if you are going out to eat for every meal. This of course can go both ways. Let's be honest, we've all gotten a little too excited at the open-air market and bought food that became hostel free-for-alls, or worse, spoiled before eaten.

  Budgeting meals and groceries will go a long way, no matter what ratio of cooking versus dining out you decide is right for you. The money you save thanks to your careful planning endeavors can now go towards more experiences, excursions, and miles under your belt.

  To go even further on your budget, be mindful of what the local staples and luxuries are. For example, in the United States, rice and peanut butter are cheap and easy go-tos. However, in the villages of Costa Rica, peanut butter is almost inaccessible due to its high price, as is rice in Spain.

- **Time:** Different days might call for different eating habits. If you have an early tour, you likely won't want to take the time to go out for breakfast that morning. Likewise, you probably won't want to interrupt an adventure packed afternoon to search for a vegan lunch. On these days, pre-prepared meals and portable snacks are the way to go.

  If your only plan today is to stroll the city streets and read your favorite book at the local coffee shop, then leisurely searching for a lunch spot may become the highlight of the day. After all, nothing is more rewarding than finding that little gem off the beaten track.

- **Wellbeing:** It's far easier to manage your health when you cook for yourself. Eating feeds our social needs and can be a fun experience, but the food is often doused in oil, sugar, and salt which are not sustainable or healthy in excessive amounts. In addition to this, portions tend to be substantially larger than what you would put on your plate if cooking at home, leading to unnecessary caloric intake levels.

  Whether cooking in or eating out, it's important to manage your plate. This can take extra consideration while traveling as you will be eating new foods and likely be distracted by all the new people and places you are experiencing. Be sure to balance your grains, legumes, fruits, and veggies. The mantra I live by is: Paint a rainbow on your plate at every meal.

- **Benefits of Cooking VS Benefits of Eating Out:** Preparing and cooking your own meals is often the budget-friendly choice. (However, always double-check this as in some Asian countries this isn't the case.)

  You don't need to worry about whether or not your dish was truly veganized or about cross-contamination in a busy restaurant kitchen where cooks may not take your personal values as seriously as you do.

  Cooking at your accommodation's shared kitchen or with your host family is also a great way to bond with other travelers. The tradition of breaking bread together is as old as the Bible, and it is one of the oldest ways to turn a stranger into a friend.

  Another benefit of eating in is that you avoid getting ripped off. Touristy areas tend to jack up their food prices. Some locations will even have different prices for locals and tourists. Other places will serve you frozen mock-meat that you could prepare yourself for a fraction of the price.

  On the other hand, food is a huge part of culture. Recipes are passed through the generations, and both families and friendships are formed over the preparation, eating, and cleaning of meals everywhere you go. You can understand a lot about a country based on how they eat. Is the meal on your plate simple and utilitarian, or elaborate and flamboyant?

While it's true that you need to be wise to the tourist traps, it's worth paying to sample the region's cuisine and intermingle with the locals. Travelers that choose to never eat out tend to miss a lot of the cultural experience. Lone travelers needn't be shy here. Don't avoid dining out if you are alone. Get outside of your comfort zone and push yourself to go out to eat as a way to meet locals and other vegan travelers.

REBEL VEGAN TIP:

Sitting at the bar of a local eatery is a cultural experience in itself. It provides a prime people-watching position and an opportunity to connect and observe the social customs.

USE TECHNOLOGY TO YOUR ADVANTAGE[3]

Before hitting the road, take the time to download a few travel apps. A few of the most essential vegan travel apps include:

- Vegan Passport
- Happy Cow
- Google Translate
- AirVegan
- Food Monster
- VeganXpress

Check the resources section at the end of this book for descriptions of each.

Happy Cow

Other fun travel apps (not vegan-related) include Polarsteps which maps out your journey along with your uploaded pictures and travel journals, CurrencyConverter which provides a currency exchange calculator for 150 different currencies, and communication apps such as WhatsApp and Telegram that support free international text and call over Wi-Fi and data.

PREPARE MENTALLY

"People don't take trips, trips take people."
JOHN STEINBECK[4]

This is the part most people neglect when preparing for their vegan vacation. Countries are called foreign for a reason—they are strange and unfamiliar. The differences you will encounter are more than simply dialect, dance moves, and spices in the cookpot. Quality of life, cost of living, cultural expectations on dress and gender, and views on human-animal relations vary vastly from one culture to the next.

This is what makes travel such an essential and rewarding experience. The opportunity to experience new cultures and perspectives, and to find your place within and through it all, forces you to become the truest, strongest, and most humble version of yourself. It is life-changing and enhancing, and while it can be hard, it is unbelievably worth it.

As an animal-lover and compassionate human being, it is almost inevitable you will see something that makes your heart drop while traveling to new and exotic places. China still holds its annual Yulin dog meat festival, Mexico boasts the entertainment of watching cockfights, and horse abuse is overlooked for Topes, or dancing horse parades, in some Central and South American countries.

Bullfighting is legal in many areas of the world, including many Latin American countries and also southern France. But in Spain, Portugal and Mexico it is even more evident in the culture, because it's lauded and celebrated as a national sport. Bullfights in these countries are attended by thousands.

You don't have to attend a bullfight or visit a zoo to see animal abuse. Unexpected encounters with animal cruelty can sometimes be part of your everyday experience. For instance in East Asia, marine spoon worms are eaten alive in hot soup in East Asia. Many markets in developing countries display their fresh carcasses on the street for passers-by to zigzag around, nose pinched in hand.

Even in cities as sophisticated in Paris, sights can be startling. The windows of some local boucheries offer hanging fowl, animal heads, and sometimes the glimpse of a cow or pig carcass hanging in the back room.

It can be difficult to endure these scenarios, especially if you aren't prepared to encounter them.

"It does not do to leave a live dragon out of your calculations, if you live near him."
J.R.R. TOLKIEN
THE HOBBIT, OR THERE AND BACK AGAIN

So, does this mean you should skip a country or region if animal abuse and misuse are commonplace? This is an issue you are going to have to decide for yourself. Personally, I don't boycott a country solely based on their animal abuse records. I only boycott the abusive events and organizations, saving my money for the groups that are fighting for and exemplifying change. Unfortunately, no country has perfect animal relations or protection laws yet, so traveling to solely "sanctuary countries" as far as animal rights goes will be quite limiting.

It can be easy to feel shocked, disgusted, or depressed by the things you might encounter. You may find yourself angry at the society engaging in the behavior you deem unacceptable, and frankly, flat-out wrong. In these cases, it's vital to recognize that everyone has different backgrounds, and sadly some people were brought up without an example of a positive and empathetic human-animal relationship.

It isn't always the people on the ground that are the problem—it is the bigger system of normalized violence born out of the various industries using animals to make revenue.

When faced with these scenarios, remind yourself that this behavior is one you have rejected. Positive change is happening around the world, and even the worst-case scenarios are being touched by the animal rights revolution. All you can do is be an example by treating all sentient beings with compassion and keeping your money and your time away from unethical organizations, markets, and events.

When you feel really put off, have an outlet on hand. Bring a journal to write down how you feel, a sketchbook to create a better vision, or a pair of headphones so you can play music that takes you to that peaceful place.

Still feel uneasy? Volunteer during your time visiting to help make a difference in the lives of the animals being affected, and to connect with locals who care.

PACKING CHECKLISTS[5]

"When preparing to travel, lay out all your clothes and all your money. Then take half the clothes and twice the money."
SUSAN HELLER[6]

Below is a sample packing list of must-have items for your suitcase (or backpack) and carry-on. Feel free to print them out and mark off the items as you pack.

CHECK-IN LUGGAGE
- Casual clothes that are easy to roll up and pack
- One special going out outfit
- Pajamas
- Intimates
- Bathing suit (add a travel towel if needed)
- Jacket, raincoat, or sweater
- Shampoo, soap, and other hygienic items (Lush shampoo bars are vegan, cruelty-free, and TSA approved)
- Toothbrush and toothpaste
- Deodorant
- Sunscreen (Skin Cancer Foundation recommends the vegan brand Sun Bum)
- Band-aids and first-aid items
- Reusable baggies and containers for food-on-the-go
- Small cooler bag
- Vegan condiments, snacks, and supplements
- Basic cooking tools and reusable cutlery set
- Journal, sketchbook, or another personal item

DON'T FORGET YOUR CARRY-ON!

- *Rebel Vegan Travel Guide*
- Plane tickets and passport
- Pen/ paper/ extra passport photos
- Wallet with credit or debit cards and cash in local currency (All airports have currency exchanges, but it's usually more expensive at the airport)
- Glasses, contacts, and sunglasses
- Medications
- Home and car keys
- Reading material
- Phone, laptop, and other electronics
- Charging cables
- Headphones
- Travel pillow, sleeping mask, and earplugs
- Refillable water bottle
- Vegan snacks

Note: Keep photocopies of your passport/ travel docs stored safely in your main luggage in case anything happens to your carry on.

AND WITH COVID IN MIND[7]:

- Extra face masks
- Hand sanitizer (under 100 ml for carry-on bags)
- Alcohol Wipes
- Thermometer
- Gloves
- Travel insurance card/ app with Covid coverages listed
- Any required health screens (questionnaires or negative test results)
- Covid Passport or proof of vaccine, if applicable

It's finally time to get moving! Plane tickets are bought, vegan meals prepared, bags are packed, and rooms are booked.

**Your *REBEL VEGAN Travel Guide* is in your carry on.
All that's left to do is arrive.**

*"Travel light. Live light.
Spread the light. Be the light."*
YOGI BHAJAN[8]

BLUE ZONES - AN INSPIRATION

The world has a few pockets of living space that have been shown to have the most centenarians, where community members are living longer, healthier lives than the rest of us. These places were dubbed Blue Zones by National Geographic explorer and author Dan Beuttner.

There are five original documented blue zones including the Barbagia region of Sardinia, the Aegean Greek Island Ikaria, the Nicoya Peninsula of Costa Rica, the Seventh Day Adventists community in Loma Linda, California, and the archipelago Okinawa off mainland Japan. Blue Zones have also been reported in the Hunza Valley of Pakistan and Vilcabamba village in southern Ecuador where it is said that people are reaching 120 years of age.

There are nine shared characteristics that lead to the increased health and longevity in these regions which are referred to as the 'Power 9'. I've listed the characteristics and their descriptions based on Buettner's interpretation below:

- **Move Naturally.** These regions are located in environments that encourage daily movement such as hilly terrain to climb, gardens to tend, and work to be done without the use of power tools.

- **Purpose.** Studies done in combination with National Geographic found that having a reason to get up in the morning is worth up to seven years of extra life expectancy.

- **Down Shift.** Stress leads to inflammation and common illness and disease. People in blue zones take time every day to relieve themselves from the negative forms of stress that are encountered in everyday life through meditation, naps, prayer, and family gathering.

- **80% Rule.** People in Blue Zones don't eat until they're full; they eat until they're 80% full. It takes time for our stomachs to alert our brain that we have reached our optimal level of sustenance. Those who eat past the 80% full mark, end up overeating.

- **Plant Slant.** Diets in these regions consist of 95% plant-based foods and prioritizes the daily consumption of fruits, vegetables, whole grains, beans, potatoes, and healthy fats like olive oil. Meat is eaten rarely, and when it is eaten the portions are kept small.

- **Wine at Five.** People in all Blue Zones except for the Seventh Day Adventists drink alcohol moderately, yet regularly. Drinking one to two glasses of red wine each day has proven to be healthier than drinking no wine, and can even lower the risk of heart disease.

- **Belong.** Almost all centenarians (people who live to be one hundred years of age or older) report belonging to a faith-based community. What the individual believes in seems to be irrelevant- the sense of belonging is the key.

- **Loved Ones First.** Successful centenarians put their families first. Aging parents and grandparents live nearby or with their children who can help care for them. This also lends to characteristic number two- purpose.

- **Right Tribe.** The social networks of long-lived people support healthy behaviors. Smoking, obesity, happiness, and even loneliness have been shown to be contagious. Centenarians are mindful of those they choose to keep close by.

Explorer and founder of the Blue Zones, Buettner, tells us:

"The vast majority of the calories eaten in the traditional diets in the Blue Zones come from plant-based whole foods. Grains, greens, nuts, and beans are the four pillars of every longevity diet on Earth.

[Yet] despite the Blue Zones' common feature of isolation and independence, the American food culture, among other forces, is beginning to take root. Village markets are now selling potato chips and soda, which in my experience is replacing traditional food and drink.

As the island's ancient traditions give way before globalization, the gap between Blue Zone life spans and those of the rest of the world seems to be gradually disappearing, as the next generations of old people become less likely to live quite so long."

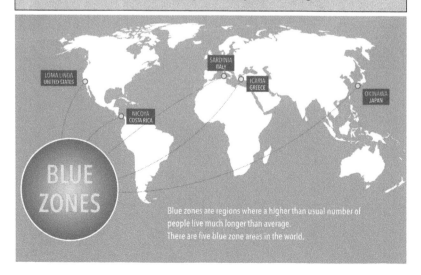

Blue zones are regions where a higher than usual number of people live much longer than average.
There are five blue zone areas in the world.

4

REBEL VEGAN TOUR
15 COUNTRY BUCKET LIST

"I haven't been everywhere, but it's on my list."
SUSAN SONTAG

Welcome to the Rebel Vegan Bucket List Tour!

It's time to begin our global vegan venture. We'll journey to fifteen awe-inspiring countries, touching each corner of the map.

I've carefully chosen these extraordinary and exotic places for several reasons. By taking a consensus of the traveling community, they tend to be the most desired destinations by intrepid world travelers. And most importantly, they have proven to me their willingness to offer vegans solid options and a warm welcome. Some locations will require more tact than others, yet in all of these destinations, we plant-based adventurers can not only survive, we can thrive. These are some of my favorite places on the planet, and I can't wait to show you around!

As we touch down in each new nation, we'll observe what makes each country special; their customs and unique challenges. We'll talk about why this is a good place to travel as a vegan, and how we can follow a healthy eating regimen while here. We will explore the top attractions and check out the most exciting, vegan-friendly cities each land has to offer. We will find festivals and events, and learn a bit of the language. Last but not least, we will find a way to give back by volunteering with a vegan-friendly organization before setting off for our next destination.

It's time to embrace adventure and start experiencing the world. I hope the journey in the following pages inspires new adventures and life-changing connections.

With so much to discover, let's start our adventure into the unknown.

INDIA: THE SACRED COW[1]

We touch down in the first country on our departure list—India.

Brace yourself; this is a land like no other and I will never forget the amazing sensory overload the first time I stepped foot on Indian soil.

From the first moment you exit the airport, you are immersed in the hustle and bustle of another world! Huge temples and shrines packed with people wearing colorful saris, bustling city streets, and vast, green nature await us, along with the other *ten million* tourists that visit this hotspot annually for vacation, business ventures, and spiritual expeditions. And everywhere the randomly roaming sacred cows.

One of the most striking differences is the sight of garbage in the streets–much more garbage than you would normally see in the streets of towns and cities in Europe or the U.S. That's because many Indians have a completely different view of garbage. Rather than keep it enclosed in garbage cans in their homes, they put it outside. To them, it's a bit odd to keep garbage inside the home.

The other prominent feature of India is its long and varied sacred history. It is evident everywhere. Known as the "land of 66,000 gods," it is no surprise that India has an almost tangible sense of religion. The countryside, the streets, and buildings are all filled with the sense that you are now in a land where hundreds of millions of people pray multiple times every day.

The landscape of India is just as diverse as India's religions, ranging from deserts to Cherrapunji, which is one of the wettest places in the world. Between these extremes, we find beaches, rolling hills, and the ice-capped Himalayan Range.

India is home to six religions: Hinduism, Islam, Christianity, Sikhism, Buddhism and Jainism. Although Hinduism is the religion that has been most often connected to India's vegetarianism and cultural respect for animals, Jainism also has a major role in that heritage—and has advocated non-violence to all beings for 2500 years.

To Jains, killing or injury to an animal or being is an act of violence, even if it is unintentional. This belief is also shared by some Hindus and Buddhists but it's how the Jains live their belief that sets them apart.

For centuries before any pandemic, Jain monks have worn masks to keep from breathing in small, airborne insects. Some monks wear belts with bells, moving their hips so the bells ring as a warning to insects and small animals that may be in their path. These same monks will walk in a peculiar shuffling motion when they walk, being careful not to lift their foot so they won't step on an unsuspecting insect.

The Jain commitment to nonviolence extends to some vegetables as well. Jains won't eat root vegetables like onions, garlic, potatoes and carrots because the plant must be killed to harvest the root. And although Jains have always eaten a vegetarian diet, modern Jain activists and scholars are advocating veganism, because of the harm done to cattle in the modern dairy industry.

WHY INDIA IS ON THE REBEL VEGAN TOUR

This country comes with a tricky stipulation but a *REBEL VEGAN* loves a challenge. India is hands-down one of the easiest countries in the world to travel as a vegetarian. In fact, about thirty-five percent of Indians are vegetarian thanks to the heavy Hindu population. While their vegetarian lifestyle helps us find veggie plates more often than meat while traveling, their reverence for their mother, the sacred cow, makes eating vegan in India slightly more difficult.

Ghee (clarified butter) and cows' milk are a primary part of both Indian cuisine and religious sacrament. In fact, India produces more milk than any other country in the world, both for drinking and bathing, as they believe the milk can purify the soul and rebalance their *doshas*—the energetic centers believed to exist in parallel to the body in the Ayurvedic religion.

Because of this belief, it makes sense that only five to ten percent of the population is vegan. However, substitutions for dairy products are becoming increasingly available at most establishments in India. And locals will likely be willing to go the extra mile to help you, as hospitality is big here. *"Atithi Devo Bhava"* is the mantra of India's tourism industry, meaning the guest is equivalent to God.

EATING VEGAN IN INDIA

Knowing how to explain what foods you can eat, what cities offer vegan-friendly options, and what ingredients to substitute can go a long way here.

Ghee can be substituted with any oil—vegetable, coconut, or mustard, for example. Paneer–the Indian version of farmer's cheese—can be replaced with tofu. Bhature and naan bread (both made with yogurt) can be replaced with simpler bread such as roti, rumali roti, tandoori roti, and puri.

Foods you can try to include are vegetable samosas, chana masala, bhindi masala, misal pav, dal chaawal, khichdi, and gobi manchurian. Vegetable biryani and pakoras are also popular Indian dishes, but you will need to make sure no ghee, meat, or other dairy products are used.

TOP CITIES TO VISIT (VEG/VEGAN-FRIENDLY RESTAURANTS)

- **Mumbai:** 163 veg/14 vegan

- **New Delhi:** 69 veg/2 vegan

- **Rishikesh:** 49 veg /1 vegan

- **Goa:** Goa is not listed, but it's famous for health retreats and hippies so it is known for being vegan-friendly.

REBEL VEGAN TIPS

If you have trouble explaining what ingredients you can or can't eat and why, you can say you follow a Jain diet. Many in India are familiar with the Jain religion, which prohibits any cruelty to animals.

NOT TO MISS

- Visit the Taj Mahal, one of the New Seven Wonders of The World.

- Try belly dancing, one of the oldest forms of dance in the world.

- Trek the Himalaya Mountains. Don't worry if you're not up to brave the summit! There are hikes way less daring than the ever-popular Everest. UNESCO World Heritage Site 'The Valley of Flowers' is a great one to try out. Wildflowers, butterflies, blue sheep, and hares grace you along this seven-hour day hike.

- See the wildlife! Bengal tigers and Himalayan bears are just two of the many exotic creatures native to India. Please search for these majestic creatures in their natural habitats, and not in cages at the zoo.

- Visit the food markets in Old Delhi.

- Retrace the steps of Julia Roberts in *Eat, Pray, Love* and stay at an ashram (The author of Eat, Pray, Love stayed in a **yoga ashram** in Ganeshpuri, a pilgrimage center outside of Mumbai (Bombay).

- See the 15,000-year-old cave paintings at Rajasthan.

- Visit the abundant temples and monasteries. Many of these require long treks to visit, but the Golden Temple at Karnataka is located within city limits.

FESTS AND EVENTS

Ahimsa Fest, the biggest vegan festival in India, was born as an initiative to spread awareness on the importance of having compassion for oneself, the environment, and animals. The fest promotes non-violence and compassionate living. There are food and product stalls, presentations, cooking demos, and parenting sessions.

Typically held: January

Website: www.theahimsafest.org

Vegan Fest India is an organization that's taken on the initiative to make the world more compassionate, clean, and healthy through art, music, and delicious food. The group doesn't hold one big festival, rather several smaller gatherings throughout the year, including poetry readings and tea parties.

Typically held: Throughout the year

Website: www.veganfestindia.com

VOLUNTEER OPPORTUNITY

Animal Aid Unlimited in Udaipur is a rescue center, hospital, and sanctuary which cares for dogs, cows, donkeys, pigs, goats, and more. And now you can too! www.animalaidunlimited.org

---

FOOD CARD - HINDI

I am vegan:

Main shaakaahaaree hoon OR मै शाकाहारी हूं

I don't eat any products coming from animals:

Main jaanavaron se aane vaale kisee bhee utpaad ko nahin khaata

---

You can check on India's current Covid status with this QR code or by visiting this link to the Ministry of Health and Family Welfare, Government of India site:

https://www.mohfw.gov.in/

PERU[2]

Next, we set off to the opposite side of the globe—and the Andes mountains on the Pacific coast of South America. Peru (and its landlocked neighbor, Bolivia) are two of my favorite places on Earth.

Both countries seem timeless and share strong and colorful customs and traditional dress handed down from their Inca roots. And somewhere in these Inca genes is the elusive cure for baldness and gray hair—I challenge you to find anyone without a jet black thick head of hair!

There is so much to see in this ancient land. We can't get our feet on the ground fast enough to go explore when we land in Peru. Floating islands, ancient archeology sites, world-class hiking, alpacas, and rainbow-painted mountains top the list of things to do and see.

WHY PERU IS ON THE REBEL VEGAN TOUR

While the cuisine here is heavily meat-based, it is still an easy country to travel as a vegan. Due to the tropical climate, tons of veggies, fruits, and grains grow in Peru and are naturally incorporated into the traditional plates. Not surprisingly, this country is home to some of the world's most nutrient-packed plant-based foods, including lucuma, camu camu, and quinoa.

Today, local people follow a mostly plant-based diet. This is partly due to economic problems, as meat is now considered a luxury item that many families can't afford. At the same time, vegan influencers have helped to spread the word about the benefits of a plant-based lifestyle, leading to more Peruvians eating plant-based by choice rather than solely out of necessity. The movement has gained so much traction that in 2014 Peru held their first vegan festival.

EATING VEGAN IN PERU

Unfortunately, animal products are in just about every dish when made traditionally. The local population doesn't eat a lot of meat in comparison to the Standard Western Diet, but they do have a bit at every meal. Luckily for us, Peru is extremely touristy, and food establishments have popped up with the sole intention of catering to foreigners. This has led to plant-based versions of the traditional Peruvian cuisine.

Foods you should try include escribano, picarones, palta a la jardinera (sin mayonesa), solterito de queso (sin queso), mango/hongo ceviche (sin ceviche), and lomo saltado (sin res y con verduras o hongos).

> **TODD'S TIPS:**
> Just be sure to avoid the Cuy that's on most tourist menus now. The guinea pig was once a traditional food that was served whole at special occasions since Inca times. Sadly, now it has become a gimmicky tourist attraction in itself.

TOP CITIES TO VISIT (VEG/VEGAN-FRIENDLY RESTAURANTS)

- **Cusco:** 47 veg / 5 vegan
- **Lima:** 118 veg / 28 vegan

EXTRA VEGAN TIPS

Keeping cultural differences in mind is imperative for traveling vegan in Peru. People here have largely depended on animals for millennia. While the indigenous people didn't eat much meat in the Andes, the Spanish conquest brought a change in diet as well as a dependence on animals for working, transporting, and creating clothes and furniture. You will see alpaca wool everywhere in your hotels and the homes you visit. Bring a sleeping bag or blanket if you don't want to sleep in wool bedding.

Wash the veggies! Raw foods can be dangerous here, as the water used to produce and prepare them doesn't meet World Health Organization standards for drinking. Use vinegar to disinfect your food before making salads and sandwiches.

NOT TO MISS

- Visit the ancient Inca site of Machu Pichu. Bonus points if you embark on the four-day trek along the Inca Trail to get there.
- Take a boat trip across the highest navigable lake in the world - Lago Titicaca.
- Visit the Amazon Rainforest at Tambopata National Reserve or Pacaya Samiria National Reserve.
- Observe the Nazca Lines - ancient geoglyphs engraved in the Earth. Skip the helicopter option and opt to climb the observation tower instead to make your expedition environmentally friendly.
- Go birding in southern Peru where the giant condors ride the morning thermals.
- Check off the fifteen historic sites of Cusco one by one with a Boleto Turistico del Cusco - the ultimate tourist pass.
- Join in the flamboyant Raymi Festival dedicated to the Sun King each June at Sacsayhuaman.

FESTS AND EVENTS

VegFest, an international festival, pairs up with the municipality of Lima each year to produce a local food fair with the aim of spreading awareness of the vegan cause.

Typically held: October

Website: www.facebook.com/VegFestLima

VOLUNTEER OPPORTUNITY

Volunteer at an animal rescue center in Cusco. While this opportunity requires a small booking fee, the organization provides housing, food, and airport taxi service in exchange for your help and care.

www.volunteerhq.org/destinations/peru/animal-care-in-cusco

FOOD CARD - SPANISH

I am vegan:
Soy vegano(a)
I don't eat any products coming from animals:
No como ningun productos animales.

You can check on Peru's current Covid status with this QR code or by visiting this link to the Peruvian Ministry of Health site:

https://www.gob.pe/pongoelhombro

TAIWAN³

Itching for some island time? Head to the East China Sea. The small island of Taiwan boasts skyscrapers, mountain peaks, and 973 miles of blue coastline bordered by white rock faces sprawling with vibrant green plant life—all visible from the plane as we touch down.

Plan ahead or cross your fingers and hope we landed at a time that will allow us to partake in one of the many colorful festivals held here annually—the Lantern Festival, Matsu Pilgrimage, Dragon Boat Festival, and International Balloon Fiesta.

WHY TAIWAN IS ON THE REBEL VEGAN TOUR

Taiwan is considered by some to be one of the top vegan-friendly countries in the world. At fourteen percent, it has the third largest population of vegetarians in the world per capita. The country is heavily Buddhist, which often coincides with a cruelty-free or vegan lifestyle.

On top of this, their forward-thinking government is pushing people to think plant-based! They strongly encourage their residents to partake in a meat-free day at least once a week.

EATING VEGAN IN TAIWAN

Taipei, the main city we fly into, is lined as far as we can see with street vendors. The morning markets offer low-priced fruits, vegetables, and soy products. We can even find vegan Chinese donuts, steamed bao, rice porridge, spicy vermicelli soup, pancakes, and milk alternatives. The night markets offer stinky tofu, deep-fried veggie goods, mochi, veggie Takoyaki, and fried sweet potato balls.

Plants Restaurant. My favorite place in Taipei that serves whole food and plant-based modern twists on classic dishes such as acai bowl, chia pudding, kale salad, and raw cakes. It's only a tiny place and the kitchen closes at 8:30 pm so come early!

10, Lane 253, Sec. 1, Fuxing South Rd, Da-an District, Taipei, Taiwan
+886-227845677

TOP CITIES TO VISIT (VEG/VEGAN-FRIENDLY RESTAURANTS)
- **Taipei:** 323 veg / 71 vegan
- **Kaohsiung:** 168 veg / 19 vegan
- **Taichung:** 162 veg / 41 vegan
- **Hsinchu:** 33 veg / 10 vegan

EXTRA VEGAN TIPS

A vegan diet here is best understood as the diet of the Buddhists and Taoists monks. Use this as a reference when trying to explain what you can and cannot eat. It's an opportunity to really live like the local monks!

NOT TO MISS
- Watch artists at the Fulong International Sand Sculpture Festival.
- See the largest work of glass art in the world in a subway station in Xinxing district.
- Visit the National Palace Museum and view as many of the 700,000 artifacts housed here as you can in one day (or two?).
- Photograph the famous Taipei 101, which held the title as the world's tallest building and the world's tallest green building until 2011.
- Visit one of the many temples, including the Tianliao Stone Temple, a Gaudi-esque interpretation of a Taoist temple built by migrant workers.
- Sip tea at a traditional Taiwanese tea house.

FESTS AND EVENTS

Vegan Frenzy Fairs are rebranding and promoting veganism on the island. They demonstrate that veganism can be connected with sustainability rather than purely religious reasons. The fairs are held in a historic house on Dihua Street. Although they are held often–there have been fourteen in the past six years alone–they are hard to plan around as they don't have a website and advertise locally. So this is your motivation to put yourself oit there and connect with the locals.

Typically held: Every 2 / 3 months/ more in the summer.
Website: They don't have one!

Ask around to get in on the action. Learn more about this and other vegan fests, such as the No Meat Fair and the Good Food Festival, at https://www.taiwan-panorama.com/ .

VOLUNTEER OPPORTUNITY

Taiwan has many volunteer opportunities on the WWOOFing platform. Be sure to find one that has an emphasis on plant-based agriculture.

www.wwooftaiwan.com

FOOD CARD - MANDARIN

I am vegan:
Wǒ shì chún sù shí zhě OR 我是純素食者
I only eat products of plant origin:
Wǒ zhǐ chī zhí wù xìng shí pǐn OR 我只吃植物性食品

You can check on Taiwan's current Covid status with this QR code or by visiting this link to the Ministry of Foreign Affairs, Republic of China, Taiwan site:

https://en.mofa.gov.tw/theme.aspx?n=2247&s=86

AUSTRALIA[4]
THE LAND DOWN UNDER

A short plane trip (or cargo boat ride if you're feeling extra adventurous) will drop us in the land down under: Australia. This is a very special stop on our tour as I lived here for two years flitting between Sydney and Melbourne and managed somehow to never be drawn into their friendly rivalry. So, I can safely say that they are well-prepared for us Rebel Vegans! One of my favorite hangouts in Sydney was at Fingers Wharf where little bars and eateries jostle together with the cruise ships on the harbor. My favorite—Alibi—has some of the best vegan food (and cocktails) in the southern hemisphere.

This country is prime for traveling sustainably. There is even a cross-continent train backpackers can take advantage of to move from one region to the next. Beaches, deserts, cities, and aboriginal culture bait every type of traveler off the boat and into the land of the Aussie.

WHY IS AUSTRALIA ON THE REBEL VEGAN TOUR?

The main language spoken is English, and it is therefore instantly easier to navigate their cuisine and explore their culture. But that isn't the reason they are on our hotspot list.

Australia is the third fastest-growing vegan market in the world. There are thousands of restaurants offering vegetarian and vegan options throughout the country, and most supermarkets have their own range of vegan foods and meat substitutes that can be purchased for cooking your own meals. And the Aussies are just so darn fun and helpful that they make every encounter a joy!

EATING VEGAN IN AUSTRALIA

There aren't many traditional foods in Australia. The closest thing to a traditional taste would be the popular pastime of cooking out— fetchingly referred to as *the barbie*, better known elsewhere as a barbecue.

Mock meat, nut cheese, and all of your other favorite vegan staples are easy to find in this country, making it as simple to eat vegan in Australia as it is at home. While we are here we can chow down on some local favorites—vegan Eggs Benedict in the morning and Gigi's vegan pizza in the evening. And of course, we can't leave Australia without trying out one of their mouth-watering vegan buffets.

TOP CITIES TO VISIT (VEG/VEGAN-FRIENDLY RESTAURANTS)

- **Melbourne:** 175 veg / 8 vegan

- **Sydney:** 941 veg / 6 vegan

- **Canberra:** 5 veg / 6 vegan - we are winning in the capital!

- **Adelaide:** 337 veg / 10 vegan

- **Brisbane:** 53 veg / 1 vegan

- **Byron Bay:** 36 veg / 6 vegan

EXTRA VEGAN TIPS

Meat and dairy aren't the only non-vegan items on the menu in this country. Beyond their kangaroo steaks, be aware that grubs, crickets, scorpions, mealworms, and ants are on the menu as well.

NOT TO MISS

- Dive or snorkel the great barrier reef at Whitsunday - one of the Seven Wonders of The Natural World. The reef stretches over fourteen degrees of latitude, encompassing both shallow and deep-water oceanic habitats. Remember to be on the lookout for the elusive great white shark!

- Venture into the Outback where you can see kangaroos, camels, crocodiles, and of course seemingly endless desert.

- Hit the coast! Take a surf lesson at one of Australia's many (almost 12,000) beaches.

- Visit the Sydney Harbour_—an "aquatic playground" of beaches, gardens, and big-name attractions like the Sydney Opera House. One of my favorite things is to climb the iconic Harbor Bridge for the best views over this stunning city.

- Explore the lanes of Melbourne with its hidden bars and restaurants. I love getting lost and finding an unnamed trendy little bar in an old pharmacy!

- Hang out in the trendy surfer's paradise of Byron Bay. You might even spot locals like Chris Hemsworth or Gladiator's Russell Crowe.

FESTS AND EVENTS

Vegan Festival Adelaide is a two-day fest offering vegan food, information, and live music.

Typically held: October

Website: www.veganfestival.info

The Cruelty Free Festival held in Australian Technology Park is about opening up a space to allow for the exploration of a cruelty-free lifestyle. It only costs $5 to enter, and there are tons of opportunities to get involved. The fest is a jam-packed event with performers, speakers, demonstrations, a fashion show, speed dating, a kid's zone, and more.

Typically held: October

Website: www.animalsaustralia.org/events

VOLUNTEER OPPORTUNITY

Volunteer with the Australian non-profit organization Vegan Community Meals. There are tons of ways to get involved here including cooking, leadership roles, and recipe creation. Alternatively, you can donate money or kitchen equipment.

https://www.alv.org.au/take-action/volunteer/

FOOD CARD - ENGLISH

No food card is needed here—we're free to focus on the sandy beaches and the outrageously cute marsupials between our yummy protein-packed meals.

You can check on Australia's current Covid status with this QR code or by visiting this link to the Australian government site:

https://www.australia.gov.au/

THAILAND⁵

The Land of a Thousand Smiles lives up to its name. Trekking through hill tribes and Monsoon forests, island hopping, thousands of crystal-blue-sea beaches, golden Buddhist temples, and lofty peaceful elephants await us in Thailand. Inspiring religion, ancient history, unique culture, a thriving party scene, and breath-taking natural features—whatever it is you travel for, you can find it here.

WHY IS THAILAND ON THE REBEL VEGAN TOUR?

As we've learned on our journey so far, most countries present some obstacles to ensuring your plate comes totally cruelty-free. Thailand is no exception.

Here, due to mass tourism, the words vegetarian and vegan have become more commonly used in recent years. The only problem is they take on slightly different meanings. Vegetarian dishes are served without any meat chunks or pieces, although the sauces and oils are often not vegetarian at all. Nam pla (fish sauce) and gapi (shrimp paste) are the salt and seasoning of almost every dish here. As most restaurants cook their menu to-order, you might have some luck asking for your plate without these ingredients, but you will certainly face some difficulties. Use your vegan food cards here and spread the word.

Why is Thailand considered a hotspot then? We can thank the monks for this one. Buddhist monks follow a strict vegan diet. For them, this means no animal or seafood products, as well as no foods believed to lead to anger or passion such as garlic, onions, chives, scallions, or leeks. Also banned from the monk's menu is honey, alcohol, and tobacco.

How does this help us travelers? This leads us to the Jae symbol, which looks like a red seventeen on a flat yellow backdrop. This symbol is placed on vegan foods as well as outside restaurants serving Buddhist vegan food buffet-style at rates even the skimpiest of travelers can afford.

EATING VEGAN IN THAILAND

Thailand is a great country for buying fresh fruits, vegetables, noodles, and rice dishes. Try out the mango sticky rice, noodle soup, vegan fruit shakes, vegan pad Thai, green curry, and green papaya salad.

TOP CITIES TO VISIT (VEG/VEGAN-FRIENDLY RESTAURANTS)

- **Bangkok:** 457 veg / 93 vegan

- **Chiang Mai:** 240 veg / 42 vegan

- **Koh Phangan:** 16 veg / 14 vegan

- **Phuket:** 19 / 25 - vegan

EXTRA VEGAN TIPS

Look for the vegan hubs. Many cities have vegan-friendly restaurants and shops. If you find one of these hubs, you can network with the employees and other visitors to find the rest. You will always see me flirting/networking with the locals - all in the name of research! To start you off, look for Broccoli Revolution on Sukhumvit Road in Bangkok near the Thong Lo BTS station.

PLANT POWER: SAME SAME, BUT DIFFERENT

I have always been fascinated by the widespread belief through Thailand that certain plants provoke or trigger strong emotions. It is always fun to rummage around Thailand's local markets as the traders do the hard sell by explaining the hidden benefits of their garden greens.

They have their 'natural viagra' in their much used Black Galingale, a root from the same family of tree as the ginseng plant. But it is not saved for specific occasions where it might be required. Often I see it on menus in various dishes. I put it in my curries and only tell people afterwards that they have had their daily dose of natural viagra!

Then there is the more sinister use of particular herbs in a ritualistic ceremony that my friends quickly point out only happens in the countryside. Here a mix of mostly dried chilis and salts is burnt with an item or photo from a person to put a curse on someone who has wronged you. It is the last stand of a spurned lover and their version of the voodoo doll.

There is a long-established history of using natural remedies: Bermamont and lemongrass for a sore throat or cold; Goji berries to keep you youthful and improve eyesight; Ginkgo for brain power and memory. These I will happily add to any of my Thai curries!

Thailand is rightly famous for its sprawling markets, and every town has one. Most of them in Bangkok are very touristy, but I still recommend Chatuchak Weekend Market at the very end of their MRT metro system. At 35 acres, it's the largest outdoor market in the world. You can easily pick up any of the above items and have a great day out of the city. And never go to any market without trying their Coconut Ice Cream. It is easily the most popular Thai dessert, accidentally vegan, and only 50 baht ($1.50).

Getting to Chatuchak Market by MRT: Take the Subway to Chatuchak Park MRT Station and leave out Exit 1, following the signs or crowds to the market.

NOT TO MISS

- Go island-hopping. Thailand has over 300 islands to explore, so get off the bus and onto the ferry.
- Watch the sunset over the ocean, and then take a dive into the bioluminescent sea.
- Ride a tuk-tuk, a three-wheel open-air taxi. (Be warned and know what is a fair price as they are notorious for ripping off those fresh-off-the-plane tourists.)
- Visit a floating market. The most famous, Damnoen Saduak, is just sixty miles outside of Bangkok.
- Go out on Khaosan Road. This is a traveler epicenter where you can grab beers, buy a cheap massage, and shop for clothing. It's where both the novel and movie The Beach starts and Leonardo DiCaprio wakes up next to a dead man. But it's always a buzzy atmosphere with lots to take in. This is a great place to meet other travelers, locals, or even just people watch.
- See the 147-foot Big Buddha in South Phuket. The white marble statue is quite the site, drawing in 1,000 tourists a day on average.
- Northern Thailand is a bit cooler with its countless monasteries, golden temples, and hill tribe treks. Make Chiang Mai your base and explore its heritage, markets, and legendary party scene.

FESTS AND EVENTS

The Vegetarian Festival of Thailand is held in Bangkok and Phuket.

The festival is a colorful annual event held on the 9th lunar month of the Chinese calendar, usually in October. It is a Taoist celebration that sees Thailand turn vegan for nine days,

However, please be warned, that these festivals kick off with a ritualistic carnival where there are displays of bloodletting and a parade showcasing purification traditions. You can avoid these parades where some gruesome displays may make you uncomfortable, but still enjoy the incredible vegan food on offer and the hospitality of the Thais. At the same time, the festival does celebrate the belief that abstinence from meat, and other mood-altering substances, will help obtain good health and peace of mind.

Typically held: October

Website: There is no official website, but you can learn more about the festival on the Matador Network at: www.matadornetwork.com/read/thai-vegetarian-festival-not-average-vegan-fainthearted

Free From Food Asia, also held in Bangkok, is a food exhibition focusing on free-form, organic, functional, and vegan food.

Typically held: September

Website: https://bangkok.freefromfoodexpo.com/

VOLUNTEER OPPORTUNITY

Worldpackers lists a volunteer opportunity in Samoeng to volunteer thirty hours a week in exchange for a shared dorm and three meals a day at their organic rural farmstead.

www.worldpackers.com

FOOD CARD - THAI

I am a vegan:
ฉันทานเจค่ะ

I do not eat any animal products:
ฉันไม่ทานสินค้าที่ผลิตมาจากสัตว์

No fish sauce please:
ไม่ใส่น้ำปลาค่ะ

You can check on Thailand's current Covid status with this QR code or by visiting this link to the Royal Thai Embassy (Washington DC) site:

https://thaiembdc.org/covid-19inthailand/

INDONESIA[6]

Our next stop on the *REBEL VEGAN* Bucket List Tour is only a short hop to the other side of the South China Sea. You could go overland through Malaysia, with its excellent bus services down to Singapore, where it's a commuter flight or sailboat to the birthplace of Tempe, and the country revered as being difficult for meat-eaters. Vegans eat easily in Indonesia.

I worked and stayed throughout Indonesia for over two decades, and have seen it develop and grow into a strong democracy. Indonesia is one of the most incredible places I have visited, as it's an archipelago with over 17,000 islands and over 300 languages.

Most people start with the four main islands: Sumatra (the second largest island in the world), Java, Bali, and Flores. It's on the Ring of Fire, so most islands are volcanic, with many still active and climbable. Get ready to explore ancient temples, active volcanoes, untouched waters, lively cities, and remote villages.

WHY IS INDONESIA ON THE REBEL VEGAN TOUR?

While the percentage of people actively practicing veganism is low among the populace, veganism is growing among health-conscious individuals.

There is a wide variety of vegan foods available to eat throughout Indonesia. The staple foods here include rice, sweet potato, tempeh, and tofu - making it easy to veganize just about any dish. In my opinion, Bali has some of the best vegan restaurants in the world!

EATING VEGAN IN INDONESIA

Produce stands and street vendors are your safest, and likely your cheapest, bet for vegan fare. Many food stands sell vegan dishes, and as a bonus, you can feel extra confident your plate is vegan since you can watch them prepare the dish to order.

Freshly grown and processed tempeh, fermented soybean, acar, lontong, and onde-onde are on the list of foods to try.

TOP CITIES TO VISIT (VEG/VEGAN-FRIENDLY RESTAURANTS)
- **Denpasar, Bali:** 37 veg / 7 vegan
- **Ubud, Bali:** 123 veg / 7 vegan
- **Java:** 302 veg / 79 vegan

EXTRA VEGAN TIPS

While it is easy to be vegan here, thoroughly explaining your diet is still necessary. In most places in Asia, vegan is not a well-understood word and is commonly thought to mean the same as a vegetarian. And since a plate with a tiny bit of meat for taste can be considered vegetarian in Asia, it's important to be very clear about what you can and cannot eat. Explain that even a little is too much, and say that the ingredient is haram, meaning forbidden, for you.

NOT TO MISS

- **Java:** One of the top-rated UNESCO World Heritage Sites and one of the greatest and largest Buddhist sites in the world—the ancient temple of Borobudur is well worth a visit. The last time I was there I saw Richard Gere quietly meditating. This temple was built in the eighth century and is constructed in the shape of a traditional Buddhist mandala. While at Borobudur, Don't miss out on visiting nearby Yogyakarta—an old Javanese city known for its cultural and historical offerings.
- **View Mount Bromo,** a prominent peak on the Ring of Fire, at Tengger Semeru National Park. This park is home to the Tengger people, an isolated ethnic group who trace their ancestry back to the ancient Majapahit Empire. Also in the park is Mount Semeur—the highest peak in Java.
- **Borneo:** Go national park hopping. Explore Tanjung Puting National Park in Borneo to see the world's largest population of Orangutans.
- **Flores Island:** Komodo National Park to see the famous Komodo dragons. While here, be sure to take a stroll down one of the pink sand beaches.
- **Lombok:** Visit the turtle sanctuary on Gili Trawangan Island near Lombok. Strap on your snorkel and dive in to swim with the wild turtle population above an expansive coral reef. You can explore the Gili islands with a fast boat from Bali or Lombok.
- **Bali:** Bali has a very separate and unique culture to the rest of Indonesia. With its endless breaches, Hindu religion and festivals, and laid back nature, it is considered one of the top island destinations in the world. Ubud is the spiritual capital with bustling markets, yoga studios, and vegan restaurants. Visit an iconic Hindu temple set inside the Sacred Monkey Forest. If the stone-carved dragon bridges and giant long-tailed macaque statues don't make this place feel unworldly enough for you, the wild macaques running about, combined with the sight of mother nature slowly reclaiming the ground one mossy patch at a time surely will.
- **Visit the surreal landmark of Raja Ampat** where hundreds of lush cone-shaped islands sit atop sparkling turquoise water. These islands are actually aquatic caves that host some of the most biodiverse coral reefs on the planet, and of course swarms of colorful tropical fish.

FESTS AND EVENTS

Bali Vegan Festival is an annual three-day fest held in Ubud. This festival celebrates all things cruelty-free and aims to unite the community and spread a message of kindness, compassion, and love for animals and the Earth.

Typically held: April

Website: www.balispiritfestival.com

Indonesia Vegan Festival at Jakarta is presented by the Indonesia Vegetarian Society, the Vegan Society of Indonesia, and is held in collaboration with the International Nature Loving Association and the World Vegan Society. The fest hosts culinary booths and talks about fostering an eco-friendly lifestyle.

Typically held: April

Website: There is no official website, but you can visit the official forum to learn more. www.worldveganorganisation.org

VOLUNTEER OPPORTUNITY

While this opportunity is not vegan-based, it is an opportunity to embrace compassion for animals. The Bali Wildlife Rescue Centre takes international volunteers to help clean beaches, restore mangroves, and care for sanctuary animals. There are also numerous dog rescues in Ubud that take volunteers. This volunteer opportunity is listed at:

www.fnpf.org/volunteer-in-indonesia/wildlife-animal-rescue-centre-bali

---

FOOD CARD - BAHASA

I am vegan:
Saya vegan

I don't eat (chicken/cheese):
Saya tidak makan (ayam/keju)

You can check on Indonesia's current Covid status with this QR code or by visiting this link to the U.S. Embassy and Consulates in Indonesia site:

https://id.usembassy.gov/u-s-citizen-services/covid-19-information/

JAPAN[7]

Amongst the Shinto shrines and cherry blossoms, the next stop on our tour finds us 3,000 miles north of Indonesia on the islands of Japan.

WHY IS JAPAN ON THE REBEL VEGAN TOUR?

Japan has hidden vegan roots under its modern meat-centered diet. In the year 675, the rearing of cattle and consumption of meat was banned due to the rapid deforestation they were experiencing, and for over two centuries during the Edo period (1603-1867) the traditional diet was plant-based. Unfortunately, most of Japan has been seduced by western culture and our fast food since the second world war.

But there are still plenty of traditional plant-based dishes for you to try while backpacking the island. In larger cities, you can also find vegan snacks and produce options at convenience stores and on most restaurant menus. Veganism is starting to take hold on the trendy Japanese who love western trends.

EATING VEGAN IN JAPAN

While veganism is still a relatively new concept here, it isn't out of the question to travel the country as a vegan. In Japanese food culture, soy is very common. Most everywhere we go, we find soy-based ice cream, milk, donuts, and sometimes even croquettes. Other plant-based dishes to try include rice with tempeh and ume onigiri, a triangle of rice wrapped in seaweed and filled with plums.

When ordering out, be sure to check that your plate comes free of dashi (fish broth used in noodle and rice dishes) and bonito flakes (dried fish garnish).

TOP CITIES TO VISIT (VEG/VEGAN-FRIENDLY RESTAURANTS)
- **Tokyo:** 545 veg / 93 vegan

- **Kyoto:** 160 veg / 37 vegan

- **Okinawa:** 38 veg / 6 vegan (This location is also one of the world's Blue Zones mentioned in the introduction of this guide.)

EXTRA VEGAN TIPS

Japanese culture demands a high level of politeness, especially when requesting anything be changed or adapted on an order. You also need to be specific in your explanation as the term vegan, and possibly even vegetarian, will likely confuse your waiter. Because of this, you'll notice your food card is slightly more complex than some of the others in this guide. I recommend having this printed and laminated and carry it everywhere.

NOT TO MISS

- Trek the Kumano Kodo Trail—an ancient pilgrimage route that weaves through remote mountains and villages.
- Visit the many shrines and temples.
- Soak in the hot springs, or dip into an Onsen (natural hot spring) bath. These geothermal heated bath sessions are usually gender divided and enjoyed in the nude.
- See Mount Fuji and the Japanese Alps. For the brave adventurer, there is even the option to hike Mount Fuji if visiting during the summer. Trails are rated beginner through expert, ranging between eight and ten-hour round-trip journeys.
- Experience the colorful "cute" culture called kawaii in the Harajuku neighborhood of Tokyo. Be sure to get your rainbow cotton candy at the Totti Candy Factory and try on the colorful clothing at Harajuku ALTA Shopping Center.
- Indulge in the rich and varied culture still present through much of Japan today. Watch a sumo wrestling match, spot geishas, and sip matcha at a Japanese tea party.

FESTS AND EVENTS

Vegan Gourmet Festival held in Nagoya, Kyoto, and Tokyo has around seventy stalls selling varying vegan foods such as veggie burgers, curries, burritos, doughnuts, soft-serve ice cream, and more. All stalls list ingredients used so you can indulge worry-free.

Typically held: Autumn

Website: www.vegefes.com

The Okinawa Vegan Food Fest brings us to a mystical vegan forest setting. Among the trees, this festival offers food, drinks, workshops, and music in nature. The festival promotes compassion and intends to introduce people to the vegan lifestyle, while also offering a space and yummy food for those already practicing.

Typically held: November

Website: Information can be found at: www.oki-islandguide.com

VOLUNTEER OPPORTUNITY

The WorkAway platform shares an opportunity to volunteer on an organic farm and sustainability project in Kyoto, Japan. Rice, vegetables, tofu, and soy milk are offered for volunteers to make meals. The farm is not listed as a vegan organization, however, they state that their mission is to revive farmland and rural areas through organic farming and educational events while striving to bring back the traditional food system to restore the food system, health, and environment of Japan.

www.workaway.info

FOOD CARD - JAPANESE

I'm a vegan. I can't eat meat, poultry, or fish including dashi, eggs, or dairy. Thank you for understanding:

Watashi wa bīgandesu niku, toriniku, dashi, tamago, nyūseihin nado no sakana wa tabe raremasen. Rikai shite itadaki arigatōgozaimasu

OR

私はビーガンです肉、鶏肉、だし、卵、乳製品などの魚は食べられません。理解していただきありがとうございます。

You can check on Japan's current Covid status with this QR code or by visiting this link to the Covid Information and Resources, Government of Japan site:

https://corona.go.jp/en/

JAMAICA[8]

Get ready to listen to reggae and dance in the streets. In Jamaica, we can stroll picturesque beaches and swim under crashing waterfalls one day, and spend the next learning the deep and storied history of the Rastafarian people on the island of rhythm and sway.

WHY IS THIS ON THE REBEL VEGAN TOUR?

Jamaica is fast becoming a vegan hotspot. The tropical climate means there is an abundance of exotic and interesting vegetables and fruits. The food is flavorsome too, as many herbs and spices are grown locally, often wild and organic in the mountains.

Then there is the revered Rasta community, which follows a plant-based diet. You can find Rasta shacks selling yummy vegan food throughout the island. The Rasta's Ital diet is centered on a philosophy of restoring vital energy to the body—energy not found in dead flesh. I would look out for roadside huts or cafes with the Rasta's flag, and be confident you'll get a warm welcome, rum shots, and a hearty vegan meal.

EATING VEGAN IN JAMAICA

The markets are always stocked with fresh fruits and veggies, and whole food staples are easy to find. The high protein, natural meat replacement breadfruit grows naturally here. It's delicious sauteed with garlic and oil, or mashed with coconut milk and baked in banana leaves.

Other traditional tastes to try include coconut jelly water, stewed chickpeas, jerk-spiced tofu, natural fruit juices, boiled dumplings and bananas (be sure the dumplings are butter-free), ackee fruit, plantains, and calallo stew or fritters.

TOP CITIES TO VISIT (VEG/VEGAN-FRIENDLY RESTAURANTS)
- **Kingston:** 18 veg / 12 vegan
- **Ocho Rios:** 6 veg / 4 vegan
- **Negril:** 9 veg / 2 vegan

EXTRA VEGAN TIPS

Meat and eggs are scarcely included in traditional meals, but watch out for fish and dairy. Try to focus on the slow-cooking locally owned restaurants. The fast-food places are heavily oriented towards meat eaters.

NOT TO MISS

- Visit Bob Marley's house, which is now a museum and National Heritage Site.

- Go bamboo rafting on the Martha Bae River.

- Visit one of the many indigenous villages to get a glimpse into the true culture of the Jamaican island.

- View the expansive waterfalls at Dunn's River Falls and Park outside Ochos Rios.

- Swim at luxurious white sand beaches across the island.

FESTS AND EVENTS

As of yet, no vegan festivals in Jamaica are being widely publicized. This is a great opportunity to embrace your adventurous side. Dive into the local vegan scene and search one out during your time here.

VOLUNTEER OPPORTUNITY

Many cool opportunities are listed on Volunteer World including immersing yourself in a Rastafarian Village near Montego Bay. Although this is only offered at certain times through the year, volunteers will take on a support role, learning what it takes to keep the village functioning on a day-to-day basis. Help out in areas of wellness, farming, music, arts, culture, and event planning. No meat is allowed within the village. Volunteers pay a fee to cover housing, and are provided with a daily breakfast and lunch consisting of fruits, vegetables, nuts, peas, beans, herbs, and spices.

https://www.volunteerworld.com/en/filter?f%5BcC%5D=388

FOOD CARD—ENGLISH

You won't need your food card here, as the official language of Jamaica is English.

However, some research before visiting might still be useful, as most people here speak Patwa (patois)—a non-formal language that is a mashup of English, Creole, and French.

You can check on Jamaica's current Covid status with this QR code or by visiting this link to the Ministry of Health and Wellness, Government of Jamaica site:

https://jamcovid19.moh.gov.jm/

NEW ZEALAND[9]

New Zealand never disappoints as it has one of the most dramatic island landscapes, intense sporting traditions, modern city breaks, and some of the friendliest people I have ever had the pleasure to meet.

I highly recommend renting a motorhome (or RV or Caravan or whatever version you prefer) so you can explore the incredible scenery at your own pace. The roads are incredible, and the signs are in English. I once spent six weeks exploring the two main islands and still want to go back for more.

Along with insights into the unique culture of the indigenous Māori people, glacial mountains and long sandy beaches lure us off the boat and into a land deemed by many to be right out of a fantasy novel. And today, it actually is the backdrop of the fantasy movie trilogy, Lord of the Rings.

WHY IS NEW ZEALAND ON THE REBEL VEGAN TOUR?

Vegan food was named a top restaurant trend for the country in 2018. In 2019, the number of people choosing meat-free diets rose by fifteen percent. Finally, in 2020, the website Vegconomist published a study stating that New Zealand is now the fifth most vegan country in the world. Many of the chain eateries here now offer vegan alternatives, and companies are producing new and innovative vegan products like plant meat made from hemp protein.

EATING VEGAN IN NEW ZEALAND

Kumara (sweet potato) was a staple of the Māori people prior to the arrival of Europeans. It is still a very popular food today and a great go-to for the vegan traveler. In addition to this, vegan travelers will delight in New Zealand's restaurant and grocery offerings. Vegan food of all ethnicities is available, and there are even fully vegan grocery shops and eateries across the country.

TOP CITIES TO VISIT (VEG/VEGAN-FRIENDLY RESTAURANTS)

- **Auckland:** 235 veg / 16 vegan
- **Queenstown:** 41 veg / 1 vegan
- **Wellington:** 89 veg / 8 vegan
- **Dunedin:** 45 veg / 3 vegan

EXTRA VEGAN TIPS

New Zealand remains proud of its world-famous lamb and seafood. While driving my camper-van around the scenic south island, I definitely encountered more sheep than Kiwis! Fish and lamb are widely available in New Zealand—in the meat pies, the stews, and the center on most plates. While it's easy to find vegan options in the urban regions of this country, it will sometimes take some patience and thumbing through the menu once you go off the beaten track.

Remember not to get frustrated when this happens, and focus on the positive—there will be a vegan entrée available. And luckily, Kiwis are friendly and helpful in finding alternatives.

NOT TO MISS

- **Journey through Middle-Earth** while following in the footsteps of your favorite Lord of the Rings character. With more than 150 filming locations, you can make this an entire backpacking adventure.

- **Walk around or boat through the Milford Sound** - rated as the third most beautiful fjord in the world by Thrillist.

- **Take a dip in the thermal pools** of Rotorua, located within the Rotorua National Park.

- **For the adrenaline junkies**: Bungee jumping at its original home. The world's first commercial bungy jumping operation, with a jump from the historic Kawarau Bridge near Queenstown.

- **View the sea life.** Seals, whales, and dolphins are commonly spotted on the Pacific and the Tasman Sea.

- **Drive the Volcanic Loop Highway** to see the lava flows along the Ring of Fire.

FESTS AND EVENTS

Vegan Expo in Christchurch and Whangarei lets attendees taste, listen, and shop everything vegan.

Typically held: November

Website: www.veganexpo.co.nz

Auckland Vegan Food Festival is hosted by the food truck collective. This annual food fest also has an eco-marketplace with locally made crafts, plant-based health and beauty products, and ethical clothing and accessories for sale.

Typically held: April

Website: www.facebook.com/aklveganfoodfest

VOLUNTEER OPPORTUNITY

There is an abundance of volunteer opportunities in New Zealand, from farm sanctuaries to working with the Vegan Society. One farm sanctuary taking volunteers is The Black Sheep Animal Sanctuary. They take live-in volunteers in exchange for food, accommodation, and animal caresses.

www.theblacksheep.org.nz

> ### FOOD CARD - ENGLISH
>
> The official and predominant language here is English, so no food card is needed.

You can check on New Zealand's current Covid status with this QR code or by visiting this link to the Unite Against Covid, Government of New Zealand site:

https://covid19.govt.nz/

PORTUGAL[10]

We are greeted by a country of wonders when arriving in Portugal. Blue-green water borders warm sandy beaches on the long Atlantic coastline. Moving inland, we cross rugged mountains cut out of deep, forested valleys to find the rolling plains made up of vast vineyards, picturesque villages, medieval castles, and more.

WHY IS PORTUGAL ON THE REBEL VEGAN BUCKETLIST?

Veganism is not very popular in Portugal, yet the activist scene is active and involved. The Portugal Vegetarian society focuses on campaigning and informing people about veganism, as well as promoting the rights of the vegan population. They've made strides that are enticing vegans from around the world to visit, and hopefully copy their efforts back home.

In 2017, a law was implemented that all public buildings are legally required to serve plant-based food. They even have a few vegan accommodations, a favorite being Honey House Eco-Retreat outside the historic village of Melo in the Serra de Estrela Natural Park. This vegan retreat offers vegan meals, natural pools, and the opportunity to practice reiki, yoga, meditation, and animal communication.

EATING VEGAN IN PORTUGAL

Many traditional dishes in Portugal are accidentally vegan. Gazpacho without cheese or added cream, sopa de cenoura, sopa de feijoa, migas de feijoa fradge, and marzipan are all traditionally served vegan.

TOP CITIES TO VISIT (VEG/VEGAN-FRIENDLY RESTAURANTS)
- **Lisbon:** 242 veg / 39 vegan
- **Porto:** 134 veg / 19 vegan

EXTRA VEGAN TIPS

Remember that tapas are in Spain. If you're looking for a snack or light bite in Portugal, ask for petiscos at the cafes or tascas in traditional taverns. Accidentally plant-based petiscos are torricada (ask for no fish or cheese toppings), milho frito (made with veggie oil instead of butter), and tremocos.

NOT TO MISS

- **Join a protest.** Portugal has made leaps and bounds with the quality of life offered to vegans in their country. Get in on the action while visiting.

- **Take in the architecture.** Romanesque, Gothic, Portuguese Renaissance, and Baroque are just a few of the many styles you'll encounter.

- **Drink some wine.** Portugal's vineyards are the eighth largest in the world, with 224 thousand hectares dedicated to growing grapes. Portugal is also the only place in the world that can produce authentic port wine.

- **Find Monsanta**—a medieval village of about 1,000 people that is built around a giant stone outcropping. Be sure to check out the nearby abandoned castle at Sortelha.

- **See the waterfall of the Azores**, a volcanic archipelago in the mid-Atlantic Ocean.

- **Swim next to Belem tower.** This fort built in the ocean served as the ceremonial gateway to Lisbon for 16th-century explorers.

FESTS AND EVENTS

Veggie World, also known as Lisbon Vegan Fest, has food, cosmetics, clothing, household items, and vegan tourism booths.

Typically held: May

Website: www.veggieworld.eco

VOLUNTEER OPPORTUNITY

The web database on the Voluntouring platform lists a vegan volunteering opportunity at an off-grid project in Portugal. Help with building, gardening, and more in exchange for a room in a treehouse or camper, and access to a fully vegan kitchen.

www.voluntouring.org

FOOD CARD - PORTUGUESE

I am vegan:
Eu sou vegana
Do you have any vegan options?:
Tem alguma opção vegan?

You can check on Portugal's current Covid status with this QR code or by visiting this link to the U. S. Embassy and Consulate in Portugal site:

https://pt.usembassy.gov/covid-19-information/

COSTA RICA[11]

Beautiful beaches, dense and color-splattered jungles, atmospheric cloud forests, and rolling farmlands are complemented by a laid-back populace and simple yet delicious food in the Central American country of Costa Rica.

WHY IS COSTA RICA ON THE REBEL VEGAN TOUR?

Many traditional plates are served accidentally vegan, with the staple foods being rice, beans, fruits, and veggies. In addition to this, Costa Rica is beginning to embrace veganism. In the metropolitan area around the city of San Jose and many of the beach towns, the number of vegan eaters is growing, and in turn, the number of vegan restaurants is growing too. There are even a number of vegan retreats and volunteer experiences available to choose from when visiting.

EATING VEGAN IN COSTA RICA

An easy go-to when eating out is Gallo Pinto—a plate of rice and beans seasoned with Lizano, a vegan veggie-based sauce. Another easy plate to order is the Casado Vegano. This vegan plate comes with rice, beans, veggies, salad, and plantain.

Patacones con frijoles, chips with guacamole or pico de gallo, and vegan ceviche are other common finds throughout the country. In metropolitan areas and some beach towns, western-style vegan fare such as veggie burgers, tofu, and vegan ice cream can be found as well.

TOP CITIES TO VISIT (VEG/VEGAN-FRIENDLY RESTAURANTS)

- **San Jose:** 49 veg / 10 vegan

- **Montezuma:** 7 veg / 0 vegan (While zero restaurants are listed, Sano Banano Restaurant has vegan options for breakfast, lunch, dinner, and dessert.)

- **Puerto Viejo De Talamanca:** 25 veg / 5 vegan

- **Monteverde:** 8 veg / 0 vegan (Zero restaurants are listed, however, Taco Taco has a vegan chifrijo bowl to die for.)

EXTRA VEGAN TIPS

In small or old-time establishments, many people confuse the concepts of veganism and vegetarianism. Some people don't even classify poultry as meat, and therefore think it to be vegan-friendly. Most places will accommodate your dietary needs, but you will need to explain carefully and explicitly what you can and cannot eat.

Bonus tip: Find the Jamaican food joint in Puerto Viejo for slow-cooked vegan food, good vibes, and spontaneous open mic nights.

NOT TO MISS

- Hike through a misty cloud forest. There are several throughout the country, but the cloud forest of Monteverde is the most popular.

- Join a coffee and chocolate tour to indulge in the country's most prominent (and yummiest) exports.

- Visit Tortuguero, the island named after its most famous visitor - sea turtles. The entire island is a protected sanctuary where turtles can come to lay their eggs safely.

- Soak in the Rio Caliente—a geothermally heated river adjacent to the Arenal Volcano.

- Go museum-hopping in San Jose. There are several to choose from, including the Jade Museum, Gold Museum, National Museum, and the Children's Museum.

- Start chasing waterfalls. There are countless waterfalls all over the country where you can swim, dive, and slide into the tropical waters below.

FESTS AND EVENTS

Envision Festival is a fest about transformation and what it brings near Uvita on the South Pacific coast. Music, yoga classes, talks, workshops, and healing sessions are available at this festival. While this fest isn't advertised as a vegan event, the food vendors only sell vegan and vegetarian food.

Typically held: February

Website: www.envisionfestival.com

Also near Uvita is the **Costa Rican Fruit Festival**, offering vegan cuisine, unlimited coconut water, juicing, workshops, movement classes, a healing sanctuary and tea lounge, a sacred tree, uplifting music, talks about permaculture, fruit forestry, holistic health, and community building.

Typically held: August

Website: There isn't an official website, but you can learn more at www.ballenatales.com

VOLUNTEER OPPORTUNITY

Planet Costa Rica hosts a volunteer opportunity in the central valley south of Volcan Turrialba at a vegan animal rescue/organic farm. The farm hosts abandoned animals including pigs, dogs, chickens, cats, horses, and goats.

www.gooverseas.com

FOOD CARD - SPANISH

I am a vegan:
Soy vegano (male speaker) / Soy vegana (female speaker)
I do not eat meat:
Yo no como carne
Is there milk? Butter? Cheese? Meat?:
Hay leche? Mantequilla? Queso? Carne?

You can check on Costa Rica's current Covid status with this QR code or by visiting this link to the U.S. Embassy in Costa Rica site:

https://cr.usembassy.gov/covid-19-information/

ITALY[12]

Italy has a big personality and isn't shy about it's many charms. With it's long Mediterranean coastline, it has left a huge stamp on Western culture and cuisine.

Although I have been to Italy countless times, I still feel the need to return, discover more of it's charms. My first trip to Europe involved landing at Venice airport in the middle of the night and roaming the rain soaked deserted alleyways and squares until the light crept up over the Grand Canal. For a brief time, the ancient city was all mine and I remember sitting by the Rialto Bridge as the city came alive at dawn. Then I took the train from the north to the Bay of Naples. I stopped off at the iconic leaning tower of Pisa for the obligatory photo, fell in love in Florence, and carried on to visit Pompeii. It was my first big trip abroad and I haven't stopped exploring since.

Today, historic architecture, famous landmarks, and their legendary food draws travelers to Italy from all over the world. Luckily for us, vegans don't have to miss out on this tasty destination.

WHY IS ITALY ON THE REBEL VEGAN TOUR?

The foundation of Italian food is cucina povera, or food of the poor, which is mostly plants. Back before the industrial revolution, a rich food culture was built based on soups, casseroles, and hearty dishes made of legumes.

While Italian cuisine varies from region to region today, it is still common for olive oil to be the cooking fat of choice. This means travelers rarely have to worry about butter or other animal products being used in the cooking process.

EATING VEGAN IN ITALY

Unfortunately, the fresh pasta this region is famous for containing eggs. However, vegans can find dried pasta made vegan. On the other hand, the traditional pizza is made vegan, as the original pizza was made cheese-free!

Other dishes to try include orecchiette con cime di rapa, bruschetta al pomodoro, and polenta.

TOP CITIES TO VISIT (VEG/VEGAN-FRIENDLY RESTAURANTS)

- **Rome:** 216 veg / 17 vegan

- **Florence:** 84 veg / 12 vegan

- **Venice:** 82 veg / 2 vegan

- **Naples:** 37 veg / 4 vegan

- **Milan:** 194 veg / 20 vegan

EXTRA VEGAN TIPS

When ordering out, order your dinner senza formaggio, without cheese, to ensure your plate comes guilt-free.

NOT TO MISS

- Italian train journeys are both scenic and a great way to meet the locals who jump on at every stop. The Italian train system is **efficient and one** of the least expensive in Europe. Ferrovie dello Stato Italiane runs trains under the brand name Trenitalia, operating a large network across the country.

- Tour the most popular destinations, including the Colosseum, the ruins of Pompeii, and the Leaning Tower of Pisa.

- Take a gondola ride along the canals of Venice.

- Visit the historic and authentic village of Volterra in the Tuscany region. While here, be sure to check out some of the region's castles.

- Stay in cliffside villages overlooking the Mediterranean Sea.

- Visit the Vatican to see the Sistine Chapel.

FESTS AND EVENTS

Vegan Fest Milano promotes the idea that no living being is worth more than another, and that we all have the right to be free and live a satisfactory life. Food, drinks, workshops, and seminars fill the agenda. There is also a bar, a kid's zone, movies, lectures, music, and activism opportunities.

Typically held: May

Website: https://www.miveg.org/

VeganFest Bologna is a four-day event intended to explore the latest organic and eco-friendly products and companies. There is a conference area with displays, book presentations, cooking demos, talks, and workshops.

Typically held: September

Website: There isn't an official website, but you can learn more at www.vegansociety.com/whats-new/events/vegan-fest-bologna

VOLUNTEER OPPORTUNITY

The webpage Helpstay lists a work exchange opportunity at a vegan hostel in Venice. They are looking for fellow vegans to come help out, share their experiences, and educate the guests about veganism.

www.helpstay.com

FOOD CARD - ITALIAN

I'm vegan:

Sono vegana

I don't eat any animal products:

Non mangio prodotti di origine animale

You can check on Italy's current Covid status with this QR code or by visiting this link to the Ministry of Health, Government of Italy site:

https://www.salute.gov.it/portale/nuovocoronavirus/homeNuovoCoronavirus.jsp?lingua=english

VIETNAM[13]

I work and travel a lot in southeast Asia, but Vietnam has a unique and strong identity that distinguishes itself. On arrival, you sense the energy flow of its youthful population of 96 million people. And most of them seem to be on their motorbikes! The Reunification Express covers the length of the country. Although not always on time, the trains are much better than in India and, if you book a bed on the night trains, you can wake up in a new city each morning. My favorite stop is always Hoi An. This small colonial town is a living museum with its timeless allies and temples. It also has the best tailors in Asia. I never fail to leave without a new suit.

Palm-fringed beaches, timeless villages, and dense, bustling cities—we can find it all in Vietnam. Vendors selling fruits and veggies are found everywhere, and vegans can revel in the unique experience of buying their produce from vendors on bicycles or floating by on boats.

WHY IS VIETNAM ON THE REBEL VEGAN TOUR?

Vietnam's history of Buddhism has deeply influenced the national cuisine. Many Vietnamese dishes can easily be modified to meet your food needs, or are already accidentally vegan. Restaurants and food stalls clearly label their food products as vegan-friendly, and mock meats are available.

EATING VEGAN IN VIETNAM

There is an incredible variety of food to try here. Favorites include dau sot ca chua, pho chay, banh mi with tofu or vegetables, goi cuon with tofu, and banh it tran without meat.

Be sure to always ask for your plate without meat toppings and fish sauce.

TOP CITIES TO VISIT (VEG/VEGAN-FRIENDLY RESTAURANTS)
- **Hanoi:** 168 veg / 50 vegan
- **Hoi An:** 78 veg / 16 vegan
- **Hue:** 48 veg / 14 vegan

EXTRA REBEL VEGAN TIPS

The basic Vietnamese coffee is not vegan, as the coffee beans are soaked in butter and/or fish sauce prior to distribution.

Beware that displays of meat and poor animal welfare are common here. Rural areas may also be lacking in a variety of veggies, tofu, and rice.

Todd's Top Tips:

Need a new wardrobe?

One of the most beautiful towns in Vietnam also happens to be home to the best tailors in Asia.

Hoi An has a timeless quality with its beautiful colonial buildings and colorful lanterns.

My trusted tailors are Yaly, but each street has several to pick from. You can choose a new design and the fabric or copy one of your favorite pieces.

It's such a luxurious treat to be fitted for a tailored piece of clothing and very affordable in this little town.

NOT TO MISS

- **Explore the Phong Nha Cave System,** including the biggest cave in the world. Within these huge caves are a water grotto with their own jungle ecosystems growing inside.

- Visit the Cu Chi tunnels used by the Viet Cong in the Vietnam war.

- **Tour the imperial city** of Hue.

- **Photograph the iconic ruins** taken over by nature at My Son, a (once) 4th-century temple.

- **Stroll the food markets** and indulge in the local fare.

FESTS AND EVENTS

The Vegan Living Fair, **Ngay Hoi Thuan Chay**, in Saigon, is a bilingual vegan festival encouraging a plant-based lifestyle. It is a free event with businesses, chefs, fitness promoters, food and beverage outlets, health and wellness experts, celebrity guests, and book signings.

Typically held: November

Website: www.facebook.com/saigonveganfestival

VOLUNTEER OPPORTUNITY

Vietnam Animal Aid and Rescue is a sanctuary for dogs, cats, and some farm animals in Hoi An. They take volunteers to help with the animals and aide in vegan advocacy.
www.vnanimalaid.org

FOOD CARD - VIETNAMESE

I am vegan = Tôi ăn chay

Sorry, but I don't eat any animal products (even honey, milk, butter, egg, fish and seafood) = Xin lỗi nhưng tôi không ăn các sản phẩm từ động vật (bao gồm mật ong, sữa, bơ, trứng, cá và hải sản)

You can check on Vietnam's current Covid status with this QR code or by visiting this link to the U.S. Embassy and Consulate in Vietnam site:

https://vn.usembassy.gov/u-s-citizen-services/covid-19-information/

IRELAND[14]

Stroll through the charming countryside and embrace the small-town life. This place wasn't nicknamed the Emerald Isle for nothing—its unique landscape made up of expansive lush green fields, moss-covered boulders, damp peat bogs, and rolling grassy hills will astound you.

In Ireland, we will experience pub culture in Dublin, search for the mythical leprechauns and fairies still believed by many Irish to exist, and chow down on some vegan bangers and mash.

WHY IS IRELAND ON THE REBEL VEGAN BUCKETLIST?

Vegetarianism and veganism are on the rise here. The urban areas have growing vegan communities, restaurants, and health food shops. Much of the traditional food can be veganized with relative ease.

EATING VEGAN IN IRELAND

The two things that Ireland is most famous for, potatoes and Guinness beer, are vegan! Other local favorites to order include a full Irish breakfast with vegan sausages, and vegan bread and butter pudding. Be sure to order the food without butter or meat stock, and ensure you are served the new variety of Guinness.

For cooking in, visit Tesco—one of the biggest supermarket chains in Ireland. Here you can find vegan yogurts, cheeses, sausages, and other refrigerated goods.

TOP CITIES TO VISIT (VEG/VEGAN-FRIENDLY RESTAURANTS)

- **Dublin:** 158 veg / 13 vegan
- **Galway:** 46 veg / 2 vegan
- **Belfast:** 89 veg / 2 vegan

EXTRA VEGAN TIPS

Pretty much all traditional food here is non-vegan, but many places in urban centers can veganize traditional dishes for you, such as bangers and mash, toad in the hole, colcannon, and barmbrack using mock meats and nut milk. Don't order these dishes unless you can ensure they are being fully veganized, as they are traditionally full of meat and dairy.

Travelers should also be aware that wool is found everywhere here, and unfortunately, the tactics used to produce this material are traditionally cruel.

NOT TO MISS

- **Try your first warm, traditional glass of Guinness** at the Guinness Open Gate Brewery in Dublin.

- **Kiss the Blarney Stone** while touring the country's castles.

- Stop off to adore quaint yet eccentric buildings in the seaside villages along the cliff-lined **coast of Moher.**

- **Walk along the charming cobblestone streets** in Galway City.

- **Visit Connemara National Park** and view the 7,000 acres of mountain, bogs, and woodland. If you get lucky, you may even spot a fuzzy ram here.

- **Partake in a traditional St. Patrick's Day festival** every March.

FESTS AND EVENTS

Irish Vegan Festival in Belfast offers food, drinks, clothing, cosmetics, and a documentary viewing.

Typically held: April

Website: www.irishveganfestival.com

Dublin VegFest is an international festival bringing vegan food, fun, and music to Dublin year after year.

Typically held: September

Website: www.dublinvegfest.com

VOLUNTEER OPPORTUNITY

Volunteer with the Vegan Information Project, a Dublin-based all-volunteer vegan outreach group.

www.facebook.com/theveganinformationproject

FOOD CARD - ENGLISH

The official and predominant language here is English, so no food card is needed.

You can check on Ireland's current Covid status with this QR code or by visiting this link to the Official Covid-19 Information page, Government of Ireland site:

https://www.gov.ie/en/campaigns/c36c85-covid-19-coronavirus/

GREECE[15]

Greece has been at the top of my bucket list since I was a kid on the farm in Canada. Before Covid, I was leading tours called The Best of Greece and had to pinch myself every time. The ancient wonders and their stories never grow old.

Rebels and radical thinkers have been making pilgrimages to Greece for thousands of years. Whether to consult the oracle at Delphi or debate social injustice in the world's first democracy of Athens.

Present-day travelers come to Greece to not only view the home of the ancient civilization, and admire the beautiful landscape, but also to visit the diverse islands sparkling in the Mediterranean Sea. Wash down the activity-packed days with a plate of dolmas, falafel, and a feta-free Greek salad.

WHY IS GREECE ON THE REBEL VEGAN TOUR?

A big part of the traditional diet here is made up of vegetables and legumes. Meat and dairy can be common, however, they can be substituted or removed from many plates.

Veganism isn't common or well-known in Greece, and outside the big cities, people won't know the word vegan. This is especially true of the older generations. Nevertheless, the food can be easily converted to make it vegan-friendly thanks to Christian Orthodox fasting rituals, which ban animal products from meals for a period of time each year. This is referred to as nistisimo, and it is based on a vegetarian diet that excludes meat, dairy, and eggs.

Ask your server for food in accordance with nistisimo that is also free of fish products (fish eggs, clams, and cephalopods) and honey. Employees of the service industry in Greece typically understand English reasonably well, so no need to memorize this one.

EATING VEGAN IN GREECE

When choosing where to eat, determine what the "tavern" specializes in. *Tis oras*, the food of the hour, is mainly grilled meat and fish. Mageireuta, cooked food, is slow and usually takes hours to make, and is therefore pre-prepared for guests. A lot of the plates at the taverns with *mageiruta* food are accidentally vegan. They won't have a menu, but head inside and check if there is anything you can eat.

Dishes you can safely fill up on include gigantes, French fries, fava, Greek salad without feta cheese, dolmadakia (on rare occasions this is made with meat), gemista (traditionally made without meat, but in big tourist areas can include minced meat), grilled vegetables, fried vegetables, fasolakia, and fasolada. Spanakopita is sometimes made vegan.

Traditional gyros and tzatziki are not made vegan. Instead, order a patatopita with skordalia - a pita with French fries, onions, tomatoes, falafel (make sure there are no eggs used for binding the falafel) with a garlic paste for topping.

TOP CITIES TO VISIT (VEG/VEGAN-FRIENDLY RESTAURANTS)

- **Athens:** 106 veg / 15 vegan

- **Crete:** 63 veg / 2 vegan

- **Mykonos:** 24 veg / 2 vegan

- **Santorini:** 35 veg / 2 vegan

EXTRA VEGAN TIPS

Fill up on breakfast! The Greek diet tends to be most accommodating of a vegan breakfast. Luckily, this meal is typically served in large, heavy proportions. Having a hearty breakfast can help you stay full, even if you end up having to settle for a less-than-stellar lunch or dinner some days.

NOT TO MISS

- **View the ancient sites**—visit the Acropolis, seek guidance from Apollo at Delphi, sit on the fourth-century stone tiers at the Epidaurus Theater, and visit Hephaestus Temple at Agoreao Koronos Hill.

- If you're looking to get even closer to the mythical gods of Ancient Greece, **take the two-day hike to the home of the gods on top of Mount Olympus.**

- **Check out the Cycladic homes** in Santorini, a city built on top of a volcanic crater.

- **View the monasteries at Meteora.** A UNESCO World Heritage Site, these monasteries built at the top of tall, jagged rock formations look like something straight out of a Dali painting.

- **Boat to the island of Corfu,** another UNESCO World Heritage Site, and check out the elegant Italianate architecture. While here, you can hike the Corfu trail—a 220 km/ 135 mile trail cut along turquoise lagoons and climbing to scenic summits.

- **Check off yet another UNESCO site in Greece at Rhodes**, an island enclosed by a fortification system built by the Knights of St. John in the fourteenth century. The island is car free, meaning you can safely stroll the cobblestone streets on foot.

FESTS AND EVENTS

Vegan Life Festival in Athens intends to demonstrate that being vegan is easy, inexpensive, fun, and has a lot of benefits to both the individual and society. The festival features talks, workshops, informational material, a kid's activities zone, and booths containing vegan, cruelty-free products and food.

Typically held: April

Website: www.veganlife.gr

VOLUNTEER OPPORTUNITY

The Vegan Organic Network in Greece is focusing their efforts on helping the refugees in Idomeni on the border of the Former Yugoslav Republic of Macedonia. They are looking for volunteers in Athens to help with food distribution, on Chios Island to work in the kitchen, and in Idomeni for a variety of tasks.

www.veganorganic.net

> ### FOOD CARD - GREEK
>
> I am vegan:
>
> Emeh hortofágos
>
> είμαι χορτοφάγος / είμαι vegan

You can check on Greece's current Covid status with this QR code or by visiting this link to the National Public Health Organization, Government of Greece site:

https://eody.gov.gr/en/covid-19/

5

REBEL VEGAN CITY TOUR
THE WORLD'S TOP VEGAN CITY-BREAKS

Congratulations, you've just voyaged around the globe on our *REBEL VEGAN* world tour. I had fun being your guide and showing you around my favorite countries.

Now it's time to check out the vegan scenes in my carefully curated city break excursions. Many of these places make fantastic stopovers and are perfect weekend destinations.

The following twenty-one cities have been rated the top in the world for vegans by multiple sources, and I'm going to show you why.

In each city we visit, we'll learn what makes this a solid vegan-friendly destination, and any unique challenges to be aware of. We'll find out how many vegan and vegetarian-friendly restaurants there are, and which of them are on the top of my list to visit. Lastly, we'll find a fun way to connect with the local vegan scene.

Here we go - back on the road for *REBEL VEGAN's* city tour!

AMSTERDAM[1]
NETHERLANDS

"Amsterdam has more than 150 canals and 1,250 bridges, but it never seems crowded, nor bent and bitter from fleecing the tourist."
JULIE BURCHILL[2]

Amsterdam is called the city of canals, and even early explorers labeled it the "Venice of the North" due to the intricate canal system.

More recently, the Netherlands cultural capital is rebranding itself and becoming known globally for being socially and environmentally progressive.

This traffic-free city center is home to thousands of daily cyclists and environmental initiatives. So it's a natural progression that the city became one of Europe's top vegan destinations.

VEGETARIAN/VEGAN-FRIENDLY RESTAURANTS

- 721 veg / 58 vegan

WHAT TO EAT

Foods from all ethnicities and backgrounds are available here, ranging from fast-food to gourmet.

FAVORITE REBEL VEGAN RESTAURANTS

- **Vegan Junk Food Bar:** Four locations throughout the city serving vegan-everything including pizza, nachos, burgers, seafood, and cocktails.

- **Mr. and Mrs. Watson:** Plant-based cheesery and restaurant.

- **Meatless District:** Vegan food and wine in the heart of the city.

- **Ninour:** Organic and sugar-free eatery with many vegan and vegetarian dishes available.

VEGAN ACTIVITIES

The **Funky Vegan Festival** has food trucks, pop-up restaurants, and live music. Another vegan fest to attend in the city is **Vegan Food Festival Amsterdam** - a two-day experience of food, drinks, and entertainment. www.facebook.com/funkyveganofficial

ASHEVILLE
NORTH CAROLINA, USA

"Keep Asheville Weird."
LOCAL SAYING

Asheville is about as vegan-centric a city as you can get! And it is surrounded by mountains with hiking trails and waterfalls for nature lovers. Yummy food, breweries galore, Tibetan shop after Tibetan shop, and city-park buskers await us in this quaint downtown.

"Keep Asheville Weird" is the slogan here—perfectly describing this hippie filled city.

VEGETARIAN/VEGAN-FRIENDLY RESTAURANTS

- 76 veg / 2 vegan (There may only be two vegan restaurants listed on HappyCow, but you can't turn a corner here without bumping into delicious vegan food.)

WHAT TO EAT

Food of every ethnicity is available in the weird city of Asheville. Vegan tacos, southern slow-cooked food, Ethiopian delights, and more. Even the (thirty) breweries here have vegan bites available.

REBEL VEGANS' FAVORITE RESTAURANTS

- **Rosetta's:** Rosetta's kitchen and Buchi Bar offers vegan soul food to die for, and a whole line of tapped kombucha. Grab a seat at the bar-top for superb people watching on the street down below.

- **Nine Mile:** This Rasta-inspired restaurant offers vegetarian and vegan-friendly Caribbean-inspired food. Go easy on the spice level, an eight made me cry.

- **Plant:** Plant offers a diverse menu of vegan food made from scratch. Ingredients are organic and locally sourced. Even the beer and wine are vegan.

- **Trashy Vegan:** This food truck is famous in this region, and even puts on its own annual festival. Carolina-style chili, mushroom burger, and a Taco-Bell inspired beefy supreme quesadilla are some of the items you'll see on the menu. The only downside - you have to find it.

- **Sunflower Diner:** Find this diner inside the West Village Market and Deli. Vegan brunch, dinner, and carrot cake waffles await.

VEGAN ACTIVITIES

Asheville Vegan Fest happens every November.

This fest is fun, free, and even offers the opportunity to volunteer. www. ashevilleveganfest.com

AUSTIN[5]
TEXAS, USA

"There's a freedom you begin to feel the closer you get to Austin, Texas."
WILLIE NELSON[6]

You know a U.S. city is a good one when the hipsters start moving in on it, and Austin, Texas is officially overflowing with them. It's a small city of under a million that is famous for it's live music scene and friendly openness. It's become one of the most popular places to live in the US with property prices soaring.

Music and art, skyscrapers and nature, craft beer and organic vegan food - Austin has it all.

VEGETARIAN/VEGAN-FRIENDLY RESTAURANTS

- 236 veg / 18 vegan

WHAT TO EAT

All of the tasty American and ethnic food you expect to find in a big U.S. city can be found veganized here—BBQ seitan, black bean burgers, tofu tacos, and so much more.

FAVORITE REBEL VEGAN RESTAURANTS

- **Citizen Eatery:** This restaurant specializes in mock meats and cheeses. Even better, they offer breakfast all day.

- **Wasota Vegan Paradise:** A food truck in the North Loop offering West African favorites such as fried plantain and jollof rice.

- **Counter Culture:** A vegan eatery offering a variety of classic dishes, including sweet desserts. They even serve brunch on the weekends.

- **Binge Kitchen:** Southern cooking is hard to come by vegan, but this vegan joint offers it all. Some standout items on the menu include mashed potatoes and gravy, mac-and-cheese, BBQ ribs, fried chick'n, baked beans, and chocolate chip cookies.

VEGAN ACTIVITIES

Austin's **Vegandale Fest**, advertised as America's fastest growing vegan festival, offers a full day of food, music, and art to eager vegans each November.

Get your ticket early at:
www.vegandalefest.com/austin

BERLIN[7]
GERMANY

*"Berlin, the greatest cultural extravaganza that
one could imagine."*
DAVID BOWIE.

"I still keep a suitcase in Berlin."
MARLENE DIETRICH

Berlin has had a turbulent history, but its walls came down in 1989, and it has become one of the most vibrant cities in Europe. It has a young and flourishing cultural scene, world-famous nightlife, and lots of green spaces to explore.

As of 2018, one in five Germans between sixteen and twenty-four are buying meat alternatives regularly. Berlin in particular has been featured in countless "World's Most Vegan Cities" lists. This is one of the most modern and fun cities in the world and you won't have to explain what vegan means. Most restaurants offer vegan and vegetarian options.

VEGETARIAN/VEGAN-FRIENDLY RESTAURANTS

- 757 veg / 98 vegan

WHAT TO EAT

Food to try while here includes vegan currywurst, obatzda dip, and potato pancakes with vegetables.

REBEL VEGAN'S FAVORITE RESTAURANTS

- **Brammibal's:** Vegan doughnut shop.

- **Voner:** Vegan doner kebab joint.

- **Kopps:** Gourmet brunch buffet.

- **Feel Seol Good:** Korean food.

- **Frea:** Zero-waste restaurant.

- **Forsters:** German cuisine using local and regional produce.

- **AtayaCaffe:** Berlin's highest rated vegan restaurant with African and Italian influences.

VEGAN ACTIVITIES

Berlin is home to one of the largest vegan festivals in Europe - **Veganes Sommerfest.** https://veganes-sommerfest-berlin.de/en

You can also join a vegan tour of the city. **Vegan Tours Berlin** combines a fully vegan food tour and a city tour. Check them out at: vegantoursberlin.com/en

BRIDGE TOWN[3]
BARBADOS

"It's warm, it's beautiful, it's the beach, it's my family, it's the food, it's the music. Everything feels familiar, feels right and feels safe. So, Barbados is home for me."
RIHANNA[4]

Bridge Town is an interesting city to visit because the culture is a unique blend of Afro-Caribbean and British customs. The former British colony claimed independence in 1966 but only became a republic in its own right in 2021.

The island has strong conservation efforts and is in tune with the importance of sustainability and eco-friendly travel. The land here is covered in a 300-ft deep layer of coral, and the populace is working hard to protect it.

VEGETARIAN/VEGAN-FRIENDLY RESTAURANTS

- 36 veg / 11 vegan

WHAT TO EAT

Indulge in coconut meat and water, rice, beans, cucumber salad, steamed veggies, fried plantains, and of course top it all off with delicious local made hot sauce.

REBEL VEGANS' FAVORITE RESTAURANTS

- **Chrysalis Café:** Farm-to-table restaurant with offerings for vegans and omnivores.

- **Alternative Eats:** Vegan fast-food offering Caribbean and Middle Eastern inspired food.

- **Lion's Share Café:** Organic vegan food and kombucha.

- **Plant Lyfe:** Take-out vegan Caribbean cuisine.

- **Trini Doubles Food Stall:** Food tents serving Trinidadian doubles; multiple locations.

VEGAN ACTIVITIES

Bajan Cooking Class is now fully vegan. Learn to make Cou Cou with sweet potato instead of fish, as well as other local plates. www. lickdebowlfoodtours.com

Alternatively, **tour PEG** - an eco-farm growing foods and medicinal herbs. www.pegbarbados.com

BUDAPEST[8]
HUNGARY

"Europe's most underrated big city, Budapest can be as challenging as it is enchanting."
RICK STEVES[9]

Budapest has recently become a sought-after destination due to its stunning architecture, natural beauty, and quiet pace of life.

Hungary as a whole is tricky to travel as a vegan. It's bad reputation is due to its traditionally meat-heavy diet. But it's capital city is fast developing a vegan scene and it is fun to be part of it at this early stage.

VEGETARIAN/VEGAN-FRIENDLY RESTAURANTS

- 206 veg / 31 vegan

WHAT TO EAT

Many stews, sauces, pastas, and side-dishes in Hungary are accidentally vegan. A few to look out for while traveling are lángos (deep fried pita with garlic), gombapaprikás (mushroom stew with paprika), borsópörkölt (green pea stew), and krumpli (fried potatoes with parsley).

* Special mention goes to **Anke'rt** is one of Budapest's largest ruin bars with large open-air beer garden with a large vegan menu and special events. And at night time it turns into one of the cities best parties! https://www.ruinbarsbudapest.com/ankert/

FAVORITE REBEL VEGAN RESTAURANTS

- **Napfenyes:** The most famous vegan restaurant in Budapest serving traditional plates.
- **Vegan Love:** Vegan burger joint.
- **Mennyorszag Szive:** Small shop and restaurant serving international cuisines.
- **Tokmag Vegan Street Food:** Restaurant offering burgers, sandwiches, and soups.
- **Fill Good:** Vegan Hungarian bakery serving cinnamon rolls, sourdough breads, Roman-style rustic pizza, and more.
- **Vegazzi** is a popular vegan pizzeria as well! https://vegazzi.hu/

VEGAN ACTIVITIES

It's worth organizing your visit so you can experience the monthly vegan pop-up market to shop for cruelty-free food, clothing, and home goods. It is held at Anker't Ruin Bar and it's where the Hungarian vegan community comes out to play.

https://www.ruinbarsbudapest.com/ankert

BUENOS AIRES[10]
ARGENTINA

"Brazil was beastly but Buenos Aires the best.
Not Tiffany's, but almost."
TRUMAN CAPOTE[11]

Argentina, has traditionally been a difficult place for vegans to travel as its capital, Buenos Aires, has been called the beef capital of the world.

However, veganism is on the rise and the city is trying to shake off its reputation and embraces the vegan movement. There are new vegan restaurants and shops opening constantly and it's exciting to see the city evolve and modernize.

VEGETARIAN/VEGAN-FRIENDLY RESTAURANTS

• 156 veg / 39 vegan

WHAT TO EAT

Vegetable empanadas, ensalada complete (double check the dressing ingredients), and papas are the easiest vegan go-to on just about every menu in Buenos Aires. Veganized versions of other traditional plates are available widely throughout the city.

REBEL VEGANS' FAVORITE RESTAURANTS

• **Bio Solo Organico:** Fully organic restaurant with attached vegan shop.

• **La Reverde Parrillita Vegana:** Buenos Aires first vegan grill offering steaks, sandwiches, and empanadas.

• **New Custom Bar:** Vegan eatery offering American and Argentinian fare along with craft beer and other liquors.

• **Pizza Vegana:** Argentinian pizza joint using potato-cheese with multiple locations.

• **RasLok:** Vegetarian restaurant turned vegan, offering a fusion of Western, Argentinian, and Latin American based foods.

VEGAN ACTIVITIES

Kangoo Tours offers a three-hour vegan tour of the city, including vegan eateries and a street market. The tour company will even pick you up from your accommodation.
www.kangootours.wixsite.com/tours

Buenos Aires Vegan Fest, and Cosmic Vegan Fest all take place in Buenos Aires.
www.buenosairesveganfest.org / www.cosmicveganfest.it

CAIRO[12]
EGYPT

"Cairo is an exploding modern metropolis which nevertheless preserves within its heart the finest medieval city in the world..."
MICHAEL HAAG[13]

Lining the banks of the River Nile, Cairo is a mix of ancient and modern. Its Great Pyramids are the last standing of the seven wonders of the ancient world.

Surprisingly, a lot of traditional Egyptian plates are accidentally vegan, some of which are even thought to date back to ancient Egyptian times. There are multiple options for eating out, and even a festival to meet local vegans.

VEGETARIAN/VEGAN-FRIENDLY RESTAURANTS

- 33 veg / 3 vegan

WHAT TO EAT

Religious fasting requires periods of eating no meat. This food is described as being Seyami. You can use this term to help you find vegan options while out and about.

REBEL VEGANS' FAVORITE RESTAURANTS

- **Bashandy Restaurant:** Egyptian and Middle Eastern style vegan take-out.

- **Hend & El Za3eem:** Vegan koshary frequented by the locals.

- **Abu Tarek Koshary:** Egyptian street food consisting mainly of rice, pasta, lentils, and chickpeas.

- **Zooba:** Egyptian street food using homegrown, organic ingredients.

- **Bam Tooma:** Middle Eastern style restaurant established by Syrian refugees.

> **REBEL VEGAN TIP:** Alpha is the best supermarket in the city and carries Alpro vegan products from the United Kingdom. You can even find some canned mock meat in many grocery stores.
>
> There are Taamiya (Egyptian falafel) stands throughout the city that is a great lunch go-to.
>
> Gad is a popular fast food chain that makes surprisingly good vegan taamiya and pita sandwiches that are vegan.

VEGAN ACTIVITIES

Attend **Veggie Fest Cairo** to share in traditional plant-based dishes. The fest is open to vegetarians, vegans, and non-vegetarians alike. www.veggiefestcairo.blogspot.com

(This isn't the official site, but it goes into great details about the festival. Also, be sure to search YouTube for videos of the fest itself!)

CAPE TOWN[14]
SOUTH AFRICA

"Don't listen to what they say, go see."
PROVERB

Arriving in Cape Town is dramatic. I remember landing after a 15 hour flight and looking out at the sprawling metropolis dwarfed by Table Mountain and then driving through endless shanty towns into a buzzing modern city.

Cape Town is the largest city in South Africa. Stunning coastlines, towering volcanoes, and venues where you can dance the night away tempt travelers to wander around this capital city. And lucky for us, the city is ultra vegan-friendly.

VEGETARIAN/VEGAN-FRIENDLY RESTAURANTS

- 69 veg / 10 vegan

WHAT TO EAT

While a lot of traditional South African dishes are meat-based, there are a few to choose from that are accidentally vegan. One of my favorites is chakalaka, a yummy dish made up of veggies, beans, and spices. Another staple you will see all over town is a dish made of pap, porridge, and tubers.

FAVORITE REBEL VEGAN RESTAURANTS

- **Plant Café:** The first vegan eatery to appear in Cape Town, this café strives to serve delicious ethical food. Find local and international dishes.

- **The Hungry Herbivore:** A fully vegan food stand turned eatery offering a wide range of meal options. The adorable interior design and decor makes the experience all the better.

- **Lekker Vegan:** This food joint offers a guilty indulgence - fully plant-based gourmet vegan food in a chic venue. On the menu, you'll find mock burgers, "beef" sandwiches, and even the local favorite gatsby sandwich stuffed with crispy chips, veggies, and vegan meat strips.

- **The Sunshine Food Co:** The options here are limited, but the flavor is big. This small eatery serves up vegan burgers, wraps, smoothies, juices, and coffee drinks.

VEGAN ACTIVITIES

The **Vegan & Plant Powered Show**, typically held in May at the Cape Town International Convention Centre, strives to bring the vegan, plant-based, and conscious living revolution to a mainstream audience. www.vegevents.com/events/the-vegan-plantpowered-show

Generous Earth Cape Town offers single and multi-day vegan tours of the city and nearby vineyards. The experience can be booked at: www.airbnb.com/experiences/69244

LONDON[15]
ENGLAND

"Mrs Brown says that in London everyone is different, and that means anyone can fit in. I think she must be right - because although I don't look like anyone else, I really do feel at home."
PADDINGTON BEAR

This is my adopted city and made me the rebel I am today. So I am proud to say, the amount of people adhering to a plant-based diet in London has skyrocketed over the last few years.

There are multiple vegan street fairs, events, and meetups to attend, as well as loads of health stores with vegan products, zero-waste grocery stores, and raw food options.

VEGETARIAN/VEGAN-FRIENDLY RESTAURANTS

- 161 veg / 38 vegan

WHAT TO EAT

Cuisine from a range of ethnicities is available in the city of London. You can find everything from vegan roasts and fish and chips to East African wraps. On my street in north London, there are Thai, Ethiopian, Moroccan, Italian, and traditional fish and chip restaurants. And best of all, I have Mildred's, one of London's oldest vegetarian restaurants—that's gone increasingly plant-based— around the corner for special occasions.

A trip to classic Camden Market, and you can visit either my favorite vegan Thai curry stall (Vegan Thai in Stables Market) or Rudy's Vegan Diner for the best burger that I have ever tasted.

https://rudysvegan.com/

FAVORITE REBEL VEGAN RESTAURANTS

- **Temple of Seitan:** American fare including vegan burgers and chicken wings.
- **Pollen Street Social:** Michelin-star vegan restaurant.
- **Stem & Glory:** Gut-friendly food that tastes as good as it is for your health.
- **Eat of Eden:** Caribbean vegan eatery.
- **222 Vegan:** Plant-based foods from a variety of cuisines.
- **Unity Diner:** Earthling Ed's vegan restaurant in east London.

VEGAN ACTIVITIES

VegFest UK, Greater London Vegan Festival, and **Vegan Camp Out** are just a few annual vegan fests held in the city. www.vegfest.co.uk / www.greaterlondonveganfestival.com /

* www.vegancampout.co.uk isn't technically a London-based event but it's worth the couple hours train journey if you can time your visit for this spectacular weekend in mid-July. I saw Russell Brand there last year.

Visit The Ribbit Hole Vegan Hair Parlor to get your veganized cut and color. Customers taken by appointment only. www.facebook. com/veganhairsalon

Take a vegan street food tour in Camden Town with Vegan Food Tours. Book your experience at: www.veganfoodtours.com

MADRID[18]
SPAIN

"I would sooner be a foreigner in Spain than in most countries. How easy it is to make friends in Spain!"
GEORGE ORWELL[19]

Spain's capital and largest city is famous for its historic architecture, food markets, and the royal family. I love exploring its contemporary art museums, distinctive neighborhoods, and lively bar scene. It is a city full of color and life.

Madrid has a ton of vegan restaurants to choose from, with more and more popping up on a regular basis, consisting of vegan bakeries, doughnut shops, cafes, health spots, and raw-food restaurants to choose from. The quality of the food in this city is superb, and the prices won't break the bank.

VEGETARIAN/VEGAN-FRIENDLY RESTAURANTS

- 434 veg / 48 vegan

WHAT TO EAT

There are tons of accidentally vegan dishes to be found in Madrid. For breakfast, try out pan con tomate, churros, or tostada con mermelada. Dinner can be a delicious wood-fired paella or a vegetable dish like pisto or arrillada de verduras.

If you're still hungry you can sample some light bites or tapas such as patatas bravas, croquetas de setas, and espinacas con pasas.

FAVORITE REBEL VEGAN RESTAURANTS

- **Vega:** Vegetarian-vegan restaurant serving a variety of dishes made from mostly organic produce.

- **Yerbabuena:** High quality vegan gastronomy that aims to take care of your body and the environment.

- **Ecocentro:** Restaurant, store, library, buffet, meditation center, and event venue all in one.

- **Loving Hut:** Spanish-Asian fusion restaurant offering an eco-friendly experience, guidance and information for visitors and those starting on the vegan path. And dog lovers will love the pooch friendly atmosphere!

VEGAN ACTIVITIES

'**Vegan Foodies in Madrid**' is a MeetUp group geared towards meeting new people and trying new foods. www.meetup.com/Vegan-Foodie-in-Madrid

Madrid Vegan Travel, a travel agency offering concierge service to help plan your trip, offers a number of tours and experiences. Shopping excursions, tapas tours, and cooking classes are all on the list of available activities. www.madridvegantravel.com

MARRAKESH[16]
MOROCCO

"I believe that Marrakech ought to be earned as a destination. The journey is the preparation for the experience. Reaching it too fast derides it, makes it a little less easy to understand."
TAHIR SHAH, IN ARABIAN NIGHTS:
A CARAVAN OF MOROCCAN DREAMS[17]

Marrakesh, also spelled Marrakech, has a lot to offer to the adventurous vegan. I love exploring the old windy streets and endless markets or souks. Tour the old city, ride a camel through the desert, indulge in local street food, and visit the classic Hammams/ spas.

The city is filled with walled homes called Riads that you can rent on Airbnb. These townhouses are built around inner courtyards with fountains or even pools. And the riads often cater to vegans!

VEGETARIAN/VEGAN-FRIENDLY RESTAURANTS

- 34 veg / no 100% plant-based yet—but watch this space!

WHAT TO EAT

Although there are no exclusively vegan eateries in the city, there are many vegetarian restaurants that offer great vegan options. Also, a lot of their cuisine is accidentally vegan. Couscous is the staple food item, along with eggplant, chickpeas, and dates. Meat is everywhere here, but it is easy enough to grab a vegan plate or some fresh fruit off a food stand while out exploring.

FAVORITE REBEL VEGAN RESTAURANTS

- **Le Jardin:** A stunning garden café with a dynamic menu. Typical dishes you will find here include Moroccan salads, hummus plates, and vegetable tagine. Be aware that this café does serve meat products.

- **El Fenn:** A gourmet rooftop bar serving family style platters. As a bonus, you have the rare opportunity to have a cocktail with your meal, as this establishment has one of the few liquor licenses in Marrakesh.

- **La Famille:** This is one of the few restaurants in the city that doesn't serve any meat products. Adorable boho-decor meets fresh, seasonal meals at this popular food joint.

- **Earth Café:** A simple venue offering gourmet-level food. They offer vegetarian and vegan offerings, including pasta, burgers, local dishes, cakes, juices, and coffee.

- **Green Vegetarian:** Ask for their exclusively vegan menu. Their vegan burger is to die for!

VEGAN ACTIVITIES

Learn to cook with Moroccan flavors at a vegetarian and vegan cooking class. I once took a whole group here and they were wonderful accommodating us all. This experience can be booked at: https://www.houseoffusionmarrakech.com/gourmet-vegan

Here's a great blog for Vegans in Marrakesh: https://travelguide-marrakech.com/morocco-for-vegetarians-and-vegans/

PARIS[20]
FRANCE

"Paris is always a good idea."
AUDREY HEPBURN

Paris is famous for being the city of lovers. I am sure it can be romantic, but I love nothing more than exploring its treasures solo. You can get lost in the bustling museums, wander the Seine River and its markets, and watch the world go by in chic new vegan cafes that are popping up throughout the city.

Paris is the world's fashion capital, and the vegan trend has taken the city by storm. However, there are some things to be mindful of as you navigate its streets and menus—France is well known for its heavy use of butter and cheese in many dishes, and unless the menu specifies vegan, then it's wise to ask about the ingredients.

Be warned that Paris has butchers shops that sell horsemeat. All these specialist butcher shops are easily identifiable—and avoidable—as there's a neon tube of light outlining the horse head signs. And, ultimately, these are no different to all the butchers around the world selling dead animal offerings. As for snails and frog's legs, these are often on the menu for the tourists, but Paris has a vast array of new vegan and vegan-friendly restaurants and cafe bars, and it's the only place to truly appreciate the delicious French cuisine.

VEGETARIAN/VEGAN-FRIENDLY RESTAURANTS
- 540 veg / 88 vegan

WHAT TO EAT
Baguettes, sorbet, and ratatouille are all vegan by accident. Other food options in the city include Indian, Italian, Moroccan, and Turkish dishes.

FAVORITE REBEL VEGAN RESTAURANTS
- **VG Patisserie:** Gourmet vegan pastry shop specializing in French pastries.

- **Le Potager De Charlotte:** Family-run restaurant that uses seasonal products to create their dishes.

- **Jah Jah by Le Tricycle:** Afro-vegan cuisine inspired by South American and Caribbean flavors.

- **Hank Burger:** Home-made fast vegan food, gluten-free also available.

VEGAN ACTIVITIES
The **"Paris Vegan" MeetUp group** and the **"Paris Vegan" Facebook group** both host vegan events frequently. These are great ways to find new spots and meet new people during your stay. www.meetup.com/parisveganmeetup

Each September brings the **Smmmile vegan pop-up festival** offering music, food, and cooking classes in an effort to help spread the word about what the vegan lifestyle has to offer. www.smmmilefestival.com

PORTLAND[21]
OREGON, USA

"Portland is a place where you can find a community as a feminist, a vegan or a fat activist. I always think of Portland as a big little city: big enough to be interesting; little enough to be friendly."
BETH DITTO[22]

Portland is famous for being the hipster-capital of the USA. It is an eco-friendly city with a high density of delicious vegan establishments, one being a vegan mini mall where you can find clothing stores, food shops, bakeries, and even a tattoo parlor.

VEGETARIAN/VEGAN-FRIENDLY RESTAURANTS

- 530 veg / 48 vegan

WHAT TO EAT

Classic American fare and veganized international cuisine are found effortlessly in the city of Portland. Vegan-friendly eateries and grocers make it easy to eat out and cook in.

REBEL VEGANS' FAVORITE RESTAURANTS

- **Farm Spirit:** American-European fusion restaurant.
- **Epif:** Restaurant and pisco lounge inspired by the Andes region of South America.
- **HomeGrown Smoker:** Plant-based BBQ and smoked food.
- **Back to Eden Bakery Café:** Brunch with 100% gluten-free vegan food.

VEGAN ACTIVITIES

Portland VegFest, the largest vegan food festival in the Pacific Northwest, offers food, cooking classes, lectures, and more. VegOut is a two-day vegan beer and food festival. www.nwveg.org/vegfest-2021

Meet other vegans naturally when staying at **The Portland Vegan Greenhouse** in an all-vegan shared space.

PRAGUE[23]
CZECH REPUBLIC

"Prague never lets you go...
this dear little mother has sharp claws."
FRANZ KAFKA[24]

Prague is the medieval heart of Europe, and you can feel like you are in a gothic fairytale while crossing the Charles Bridge to explore its Old Town Square surrounded by castles and cathedrals. Rated in the top-ten vegan-friendly cities on multiple lists, Prague offers many vegan shopping options for food, clothing, home supplies, and more.

VEGETARIAN/VEGAN-FRIENDLY RESTAURANTS

- 231 veg / 58 vegan

WHAT TO EAT

Traditional Czech food is heavy on meat and cheese. However, many restaurants have veganized these plates so you can indulge in the potato pancakes, dumplings, grilled (veggie) sausages, and bread knedliky.

FAVORITE REBEL VEGAN RESTAURANTS

- **Moment Kayarna & Bistro**: Veganized Czech and Thai food.
- **Forrest Bistro**: Vegan bistro and espresso bar offering a homestyle menu.
- **Shromaždiště**: Vegan pub with fair prices.
- **Forky's**: Vegan fast food specializing in cheeseburgers and fries.
- **Social Bistro Střecha**: Vegan restaurant and café offering employment to those in need of a second chance due to homelessness or recent release from prisons.

VEGAN ACTIVITIES

PlanetFest is a vegan, zero-waste festival that includes a large eco-friendly vegan market. Veggie Naplavka is a bi-annual gathering that brings together over a hundred vegan and vegan-friendly retailers and restaurants. www.planetfest.cz/en

Personalized walking tours are available through the organization **I Like Veggie**. Find them at: www.airbnb.com/experiences/124091

PUERTO VALLARTA[25]
MEXICO

Pata Salada / Salty Foot is the name for the local people. If someone calls you Pata Salada, it's a huge compliment and you are embraced as a local!

Most people head to Puerto Vallarta for the all-inclusive beach resorts, but the city itself has a lot to offer. Conde Nast Traveler rates it as the world's friendliest international city.[26] On top of this, the city is known for it's laid back nature, world class restaurants, and its spectacular sunsets.

And now, it's catching the limelight for it's rise in vegan-friendly establishments.

VEGETARIAN/VEGAN-FRIENDLY RESTAURANTS

- 35 veg / 6 vegan

WHAT TO EAT

A cuisine heavy in rice, beans, and fruit makes for an easy vegan holiday. While almost every dish is traditionally cooked with meat or dairy, the local people are kind and hospitable, and can help you find ways to veganize the popular local eats.

FAVORITE REBEL VEGAN RESTAURANTS

- **Planeta Vegetariano:** This restaurant offers both vegan and vegetarian options. I recommend checking out the breakfast buffet where you can fill up on papaya, pineapple, melon, veganized chilaquiles, and warm beans.

- **Vegan Inc:** A contemporary, health-focused vegan joint offering a variety of foods including Mexican fare, American fare, sushi, and deserts. Choose between fruit juice, smoothies, or local-brewed beer.

- **Corazón Saludable:** The name of this restaurant translates to healthy heart—and their food will deliver on that promise. They offer vegan-friendly Mexican plates with two to three offerings a day.

- **La Palapa:** A Mexican-Caribbean fusion restaurant serving carnivorous, vegetarian, vegan, and gluten-free dishes—all clearly labeled.

VEGAN ACTIVITIES

Drop in on **Vegan Fiesta Mexico**, Festival de Sabores to sample authentic local flavors in vegan form. Take part in workshops, watch educational presentations, join in on a yoga or fitness class, and shop the cruelty-free market. Learn more at:
www.vallartadaily.com/vegan-festival-vallarta

SINGAPORE[27]
SOVEREIGN CITY-STATE

*"Nobody in Singapore drinks Singapore Slings.
It's one of the first things you find out there.
What you do in Singapore is eat. It's a really
food-crazy culture, where all of this great food is
available in a kind of hawker-stand environment."*
ANTHONY BOURDAIN[28]

Singapore is famous for being a super clean and green city, and it doesn't disappoint. It is also one of the richest—and most expensive—cities globally. But you can easily get cheap vegan food at its many food courts.

PETA voted Singapore as Asia's second most vegan destination, behind only Taiwan. Food markets clearly label outlets serving vegetarian and vegan food so it's easy to find something amazing while you travel.

VEGETARIAN/VEGAN-FRIENDLY RESTAURANTS
- 1,280 veg / 71 vegan

WHAT TO EAT
Foods to try while here include louts and vegetable buns, tau sar pau (red bean paste), ondeh ondeh (juice-filled cake balls), and dairy free boba tea (bubble tea).

FAVORITE REBEL VEGAN RESTAURANTS
- **Fortune Center:** Vegetarian food court.
- **Genesis:** Vegan restaurant serving local and international favorites.
- **E Veg:** Vegan halal food stalls found throughout the city.
- **Smoocht Pantry:** Vegan pizzeria and ice cream parlor.
- **Mummy Yummy:** Chinese restaurant that uses profits to feed those in need.
- **Makan Vegan:** Vegan food stall in multiple locations.
- **NomVnom Xpress:** Vegan fast-food eatery launched in 2021 that serves burgers, fries, and bubble tea.

VEGAN ACTIVITIES
AirBnB Experiences offers a vegan food walking tour of Singapore's first heritage town—Joo Chiat.
https://www.airbnb.co.uk/experiences/288158

Alternatively, head to Kechil Kitchen to learn how to cook your own vegan and vegetarian dishes with MasterChef finalist Sowmiya Venkatesan. https://www.kechilkitchen.com/

TEL AVIV[29]
ISRAEL

"A city that never sleeps."
TEL AVIV SLOGAN

Israel has the highest percentage of vegans globally, with an estimated five to eight percent of the population being vegan.

Tel Aviv is a stunning city nestled on Israel's Mediterranean coast. It is known for its old-world charm and is quickly becoming one of the world's vegan capitals.

There are two vegan grocers in the city of Tel Aviv, a men's clothing store, and a faux leather shoe/bag stop.

This is a vegan oasis!

VEGETARIAN/VEGAN-FRIENDLY RESTAURANTS

- 586 veg / 36 vegan

WHAT TO EAT

Falafel, hummus, and pita are obvious choices when it comes to vegan Israeli food. Other yummy options include sambusak, lentils, sabich (without egg), dolma, and basbousa for dessert.

REBEL VEGANS' FAVORITE RESTAURANTS

- **Zakaim Vegan Boutique:** Popular Persian and Middle Eastern diner.

- **COCO Vegan Chocolate:** Vegan chocolate shop.

- **Meshek Barzilai:** Organic vegetarian restaurant with several vegan options.

- **Simply Happy Kitchen:** Hot and ready soup bar with vegan products for sale.

- **Dosa Bar:** South Indian street food done vegan style.

VEGAN ACTIVITIES

Vegan Fest is a two-day festival with 100 stalls from the best vegan restaurants and shops, lectures, and cooking workshops. Find tickets and info at: https://www.secrettelaviv.com/tickets/vegan-fest

Vegan food tours and cooking classes are available, many of which can be booked through Viator: www.viator.com

TORONTO[30]
CANADA

"Canada is a country of ingredients without a cuisine; we're a country with musicians without an indigenous instrument; Toronto's a city that doesn't even have a dish named after it."
MIKE MYERS[31]

Toronto may not be the capital of Canada, but its still got plenty of swagger and style. And it is fast becoming a vegan food capital and it was bound to make the list—this is one of HappyCow's Top 10 vegan-friendly cities.

Indulge in multicultural shops and eat in the third biggest city of the North American continent.

VEGETARIAN/VEGAN-FRIENDLY RESTAURANTS

- 333 veg / 76 vegan

WHAT TO EAT

You can find food from all over the world here, and pretty much all of it can be veganized, from American fare and Canadian Poutine to authentic Japanese cuisine.

FAVORITE REBEL VEGAN RESTAURANTS

- **Hogtown Vegan on College:** This vegan joint offers all the best comfort food. Chow down on soy-wings, veganized poutine, phish 'n chips, unchicken and waffles, and mac n' cheez.

- **Alter Foods & Alternative Thinking:** A grab-and-go café inside a shop selling bulk foods and other vegan treats.

- **Avelo:** Gourmet vegan restaurant in the downtown area. Plates include black rice risotto, artichoke ravioli, and gnocchi with baby kale.

- **Bar Vegandale:** This restaurant partnered up with Dougan's brewery to make a truly unique vegan bar and grill. Fried jalapeno poppers, pulled pork sandwiches, Philly cheesesteak, burgers, and more - all done vegan.

- **Bloomer's:** Vegan bakery with cookies, cupcakes, pies, tarts, and doughnuts.

VEGAN ACTIVITIES

Toronto Veg Food Fest has been up and running since 1984, and is a celebration of all things veg. Learn more at: www.vegfoodfest.com

Tastecapade offers a four-hour vegan food tour in the Christie Parks neighborhood. All the places visited are local family establishments. https://www.tastecapade.com/tour/vegan-food-tour

VIENNA[32]
AUSTRIA

"The streets of Vienna are paved with culture, the streets of other cities with asphalt."
KARL KRAUS

"When you set out to take Vienna, take Vienna."
NAPOLEON BONAPARTE

Vienna has a unique charm and vibrancy. With its outstanding infrastructure and clean streets, it has been voted the most liveable city in the world many times over.

Just outside the city is the sprawling Vienna Woodlands. This range of hills is heavily forested with recreational rivers, caves, wild woodland animals & footpaths.

Vienna was catering to vegans even before it was the trendy thing to do. Their first vegan restaurant opened up way back in 1988. Vegan visitors can indulge in many Viennese plates and traditions ohne Fleisch—without meat.

VEGETARIAN/VEGAN-FRIENDLY RESTAURANTS

- 417 veg / 40 vegan

WHAT TO EAT

There are a number of traditional Austrian dishes that can be enjoyed by vegans. Veganized versions of other traditional plates can be found in spots throughout the city.

REBEL VEGANS' FAVORITE RESTAURANTS

- **Swing Kitchen:** Chain vegan restaurant where you can listen to swing music while eating; operates plastic-free.

- **Oma's Backstube:** Vegan bakery serving Viennese pastries.

- **Harvest Cafe Bistrot:** Viennese café with vintage Austrian vibe.

- **Pepper & Ginny:** Viennese delicatessen offering vegan delicacies from around the world.

VEGAN ACTIVITIES

Join an activity with one of the local MeetUp groups '**Vienna Vegans**' and '**Essential Oils & Raw Vegan & Cooking Workshops**'. www.meetup.com/Vienna-Vegans / www.meetup.com/Essential-Oils-Raw-Vegan-Cooking-Workshops

Spend a day at Veganmania - Europe's largest vegan festival, taking place each year in Vienna, Innsbruck, and Graz. Shop for food, clothes, cosmetics, cookbooks, and more. www.veganmania.at

WARSAW[33]
POLAND

"Poland has been overrun by two of the great powers which held her in bondage for 150 years but were unable to quench the spirit of the Polish nation. The heroic defense of Warsaw shows that the soul of Poland is indestructible, and that she will rise again like a rock which may for a spell be submerged by a tidal wave but which remains a rock."
WINSTON CHURCHILL[34]

Warsaw—and nearby Krakow—are fascinating places to explore. It is incredible to walk along its Golden Mile (Krakowskie Przedmiescie) towards the Presidential Palace and think this medieval city center has been rebuilt from the ground up after the extensive bombing of Worlds War Two.

Warsaw has a variety of vegan food options to choose from, covering everything from traditional Polish food to classic vegan burger chains. And the cost of traveling here is far lower than the more tourist-oriented Western European countries.

VEGETARIAN/VEGAN-FRIENDLY RESTAURANTS

- 211 veg / 64 vegan

WHAT TO EAT

Sweet and savory soups, borscht, potato pancakes with applesauce or sauerkraut (depending on your mood), and baked apples are all accidentally vegan.

Cabbage rolls in Poland are not traditionally made vegan, but the plant-based version has become rather common and can now be found in most places around Warsaw.

FAVORITE REBEL VEGAN RESTAURANTS

- **Vege Miasto:** Vegan versions of traditional Polish food along with other international dishes.

- **Leonardo Verde:** Italian food veganized.

- **Lokal Vegan Bistro:** Vegan versions of traditional Polish food in a homey atmosphere.

- **The Botanist:** Bar and restaurant that adheres to a strict vegan menu.

- **Eden Bistro:** Delectable vegan food in a picturesque setting.

VEGAN ACTIVITIES

Warsaw has a MeetUp group that you can join to meet local vegans. www.meetup.com/es/warsaw-healthy-vegan-meetup-group

Attend the Vege Festival of Warsaw. This fest embraces the vegan lifestyle by promoting many different vegan products and hosting lectures and meetings on the topic. www.facebook.com/wegefestiwal

6

STAYCATIONS
VEGANIZE LOCALLY[1]

"The whole object of travel is not to set foot on foreign land; it is at last to set foot on one's own country as a foreign land."
G. K. CHESTERTON[2]

As we emerge from lockdowns and Covid restrictions are lifted, the intrepid traveler in all of us wants to get back out there in the world, to engage and connect. While we were forced to stay at home and wait for things to blow over, we realized how much we missed our freedom to roam, experience other cultures, and trek over foreign landscapes.

However, many people feel understandably anxious or hesitant about getting back out there. Our "new normal" has left us weary of ever-changing travel restrictions. International restrictions are shifting and changing, and travelers are taking on bigger risks as borders close. With all this change, the world seems to be getting bigger and scarier, making it logical to want to start small and stay local. It is okay to test our travel boots in safer terrain - to travel our own backyards.

A wonderful solution to these worries is to ease into the travel life with a staycation—defined by Oxford dictionary as:

"A vacation spent in one's home country rather than abroad, or spent at home and involving day trips to local attractions."[3]

I know... to the intrepid traveler, the phrases staycation and ease into likely sound like nails on a chalkboard. I understand, I used to scoff at the idea of traveling close to home after having traveled continuously for fifteen years over four different continents. I didn't stop long enough to appreciate the beauty and mystery that was my native land. I had overlooked my homeland and roots.

Covid has limited all of our freedoms, but also given us a new lens to see the world. After it forced me to lockdown in London, and I spent that first long winter in the northern hemisphere, I've gained a new appreciation for my local community. I've gotten to know the local vegan scene and have had the opportunity to reconnect with my roots.

I've learned the value of the staycation.

As a first-time traveler, traveling close to home can remove a lot of the potential stress associated with "long-haul" travel. For starters, you are already familiar with the language and culture in your hometown. It will be easier to find which areas are safe, and what regions will be enjoyable for you, as you likely know other people who have visited the town or province you are wanting to travel to.

Being closer to your home and loved ones will make you feel safer in general, not to mention you're a quick journey away should something imperative come up, forcing you to end your trip early.

The staycation is a great way for new travelers to gain confidence, and for seasoned globe-trotters setting back out to brush off the rust.

WHY STAYCATION?[4]

*"Some people look for a beautiful place.
Others make a place beautiful."*
HAZRAT INAYAT KHAN

Getting your footing isn't the only reason to consider embarking on a staycation. This is an opportunity to connect to your roots, learn your history, and create a stronger home community.

Let's look at some of the other reasons you might want to start your post-pandemic journey close to home.

IMPROVE YOUR CARBON FOOTPRINT

In 2016, transport-related emissions from tourism represented five percent of all man-made emissions. Before the pandemic struck, this number was only expected to grow.

Unfortunately, many of the hottest tourist destinations that elicit emission-dumping flights are also the most sensitive climates in terms of climate change. The 11.5-billion dollars spent on travel to the coral reefs reported by the Intergovernmental Panel on Climate Change in one year is a prime example of this phenomenon.

But why does traveling close to home affect your carbon footprint? The main difference here is the distance traveled. A shorter distance means a smaller output, especially if you can ditch the airline and hop on a train instead. According to EcoPassenger, the CO_2 output caused by a trip from London to Paris (with a fully booked plane/train/or vehicle) is:

- 122 KG (or .12 tons of CO2) by plane
- 48 KG (.04 tons of CO2) by car
- 15 KG (or .01 tons of CO2) by train

SAVE MONEY

The aspect of minimal travel distance is obviously great for the environment. You'll also be happy to learn it's great for your bank account too. The hefty costs of airline tickets, rental cars, and foreign entry fees are avoided when traveling close to home.

You can also save money by packing up a cooler of food to take with you, and doing away with the purchase of the suitcase large enough to hold thirty days' worth of casual and dressy wear.

As trips close to home are often far shorter than those abroad, less time off work is required, and therefore less lost income while enjoying your home-region vacation.

PLAN FOR SMOOTH SAILING

Organizing and planning a trip close to home is typically easier than scheduling a journey abroad. Most people are more familiar with their hometown or even their neighboring province than they are with a country on the other side of the globe. Hotel names are recognizable, and the cost of services and goods is familiar.

On top of this, the planning process becomes much smoother when you can read and speak the language of the destination and call the accommodations with questions without paying international charges.

DITCH THE STRESS

It's important to find opportunities to get away from routine and the stressors of day-to-day life. For those who don't have the privilege to cross the globe in search of R&R due to government restrictions, family obligations, or a busy work life, a staycation is a great solution.

In fact, in some ways, a staycation can be less stressful than a vacation, as you don't have to navigate foreign cities or spend long hours traveling between destinations.

And it's always a plus to bypass the airport security line. The benefits of a vacation (relaxation, fun, and sightseeing) are available to us in our home communities, and it would be a shame for us to let them go to waste.

EMBRACE YOUR COMMUNITY AND CELEBRATE YOUR ROOTS

With embracing your local community comes supporting it.

Tourism is enormously important to many economies, and you can support your local and national economy by choosing to vacation at home.

We all became familiar with our local businesses and the struggles they endured during Covid. Wouldn't it be rewarding to support them with our 'tourism' dollars? I

n addition, you'll be supporting your local vegan community—helping vegan cafes, food markets, and community centers stay afloat during difficult times.

PETS INCLUDED

Bring your furry friend along, as no pet passports or special vaccinations are required.

FUN IDEAS TO TRY

There is no right or wrong way to staycation - the important thing is to do something different than you normally would. Get out and explore, or find a nice place to stay in and relax. There are tons of ways to travel close to home. Get creative and craft your ideal staycation.

Here are some fun ideas I've come across to get you started:[5]

- **Spa-Day:** Recreate a spa experience at home. Pick up fresh bath towels, scented candles, and your favorite scented bath-salt to treat yourself to a soothing bath. Spruce it up with soft music and a good book.

- **Be a Cliché-Tourist:** Check out an online tourism page for your city and start checking items off the list. You may find yourself surprised at the hidden gems your home region has to offer. This is an excellent way to try new and exciting things and discover new places to shop, eat, and play while supporting your local economy.

- **Retreat to Meditation:** Find a retreat center near you and book a weekend! Meditation, yoga, and juicing retreats seem to be the most common available - and for a reason. Mindful meditation can help clear your mind and keep you grounded in the present, reducing stress and anxiety. Yoga produces similar results with the added benefits of moderate exercise. And of course, juicing is a great vegan experiment!

- **Journey to the Kitchen:** A popular tourist activity is attending a cooking class to learn about and sample the local cuisine. Hosting a cooking night or attending a local cooking class at home are both fun and delicious ways to feel like you are traveling. It's a great opportunity to try out new vegan dishes, and unlike the cooking classes abroad, these recipes will consist of ingredients you can easily find in your local supermarket for recreating later!

- **Pitch a Tent:** Maybe you can't travel to the Alps or the Andes right now, but you can prepare by getting into the great outdoors of your local forest preserve. You could even do this in your own backyard if camping isn't available nearby. Remember to pack veggie dogs and vegan marshmallows (yes, they exist!) for roasting over the fire.

- **Book a Night Away:** Even if you can't travel to a neighboring region right now, you can still experience some time away from home. Book a locally owned hotel or bed and breakfast to truly embrace the thought of seeing your town as a tourist. This is a fun way to enjoy the small luxuries of travel without having to travel at all. This is also a sneaky way to travel for those who can't get a weekend off work to get away.

- **Get Aboard a Train:** Train journeys are always an awesome adventure. You're free to take in all the scenery or cozy up with a book along the way. Take it to the furthest place it goes, and see where you end up!

- **Rent an RV/Motorhome:** Explore what's been all around you. Use this as an opportunity to stop off at all those quirky roadside places you've always wondered about. The world's largest ball of yarn, a mountain constructed of clay and paint, or a giant hole n' the rock - you are there.

HOW TO MAKE THE MOST OF IT

"One's destination is never a place,
but a new way of seeing things."
HENRY MILLER

To really make the most of your staycation, it's best to try your hardest to stay in the mindset of being away. When on vacation, you're more likely to try new things, react positively to hiccups along the way, and ignore that pesky call after hours from work.

When staycationing, minimize electronic use. This is the easiest and most effective way to disconnect from the demands and stressors of everyday life, as your phone and laptop tend to keep you tethered to those responsibilities. Minimizing screen time will help you to better enjoy the overall travel experience.

While staying in the mindset of being away, the beauty of a staycation is that you are close to home after all. Lighten your load by only packing the necessities to avoid lugging around heavy suitcases or living in a room cluttered by unneeded luggage.

Ultimately, staycations involve a rethinking of travel and adventure, and that necessitates a shift in mindset. Let's see this as an incredible opportunity to view the world through a new lens, discover the beauty all around us, and reconnect with our roots.

And remember the *REBEL VEGAN* motto:

If you can visualize it,

You can veganize it.

MEETING YOUR IDOLS: JEREMY BENTHAM

When I first arrived in London, I made a pilgrimage to meet one of my heroes. I was not disappointed. I found Jeremy Bentham in the Student Centre of University College London (UCL), looking immaculate in his best suit and was sitting up with a smirk on his face. He was also long dead!

The wonderfully eccentric English social reformer and philosopher wrote about women's suffrage and LGBTQ+ rights when such things were not on the agenda.

Bentham (1749-1832) was also the first Western philosopher to give animals equal consideration and one of the earliest modern animal rights defenders. Whereas his colleagues in Ancient Greece made their arguments based on the moral status of animals themselves (Greek mathematician and philosopher Pythagoras made the case against eating animals because they had divine souls like humans), two thousand years later, in 1789, Jeremy Bentham framed his defense of animal welfare within a non-religious moral theory. He argued that the ability to suffer, not reason, should be the benchmark for ethical consideration. He reasoned that if intelligence alone were the baseline by which we judge who ought to have rights, young children and adults with specific disabilities might also fall short. On this basis, he argued for animal welfare legislation.

His classic quote still challenges us today:

"The question is not, Can they reason?
Nor, Can they talk? But, Can they suffer?

Why should the law refuse its protection to any sensitive being?

The time will come when humanity will extend its mantle over everything which breathes..."

Bentham was ahead of his time and cultivated his increasingly eccentric image throughout his long life. As well as being a radical thinker, he used a walking stick he called Dapple, a teapot referred to as Dickey and his cat he named The Reverend Sir John Langbourne.

But in death, Bentham was even more unusual. His last will and testament requested that his body be publicly dissected for medical research and his head and skeleton reassembled into an auto-icon so that he could be wheeled out to join friends at parties.

Today, his preserved body sits on permanent display in the middle of the bustle of the busy Student Centre at UCL. He has become the auto-icon he always wanted to be and a patron saint of animal rights. Bentham is even still invited to all College Council gatherings, where he is recorded in the minutes as 'present but not voting. He still has a lot to teach today's students and would be pleased to be invited to the party.

If you find yourself near Bloomsbury, central London, why not stop by the university and meet Bentham yourself?

(UCL Student Centre, 27-28 Gordon Square, London WC1H 0AH)

7

CONNECTIONS
FINDING YOUR COMMUNITY[1]

"Drink heavily with locals whenever possible."
ANTHONY BOURDAIN[2]

Everything seems to be falling into place. You've picked your dream destination and mastered how to plan, pack, and put in motion the perfect plant-based adventure. With your vegan food-cards, the directory of resources and recipes provided to you in this guide, you are ready to take on the world.

There is a wonderful sense of confidence and contentment when embracing a life in line with your values. How we eat and travel has never mattered more and we are leading the way in building a better world.

However, especially when traveling to unknown places, we all yearn to connect, to be part of something, to belong. A rebel needs to find their comrades!

In the following chapter, we are going to touch on the possible roadblocks, potholes, and other obstacles that may cause unexpected turbulence in your travels. But first, I want to help you overcome the biggest bump in the road you'll likely encounter as a vegan, because whether we are at home or on the road, we all need to find our tribe.

According to the US Humane Research Council, 84% of vegans and vegetarians quit the lifestyle, half of these during the first year. One of the top reasons listed was that people weren't involved socially with other veg folks.[3]

We are social creatures—connection and a sense of belonging are imperative to our success and happiness. Maslow's hierarchy of needs lists "belongingness" as the first of the psychological needs, preceded only by the basic needs of food, water, rest, and physical safety.[4]

Contrary to popular belief, traveling vegan doesn't restrict your opportunities. Being vegan widens the world for the vegan traveler. Veganism opens the door to a ready-made community of people who by default share similar values, ethics, and meals as you.

This is especially handy for the solo traveler. Once, I found my tribe at a small vegan café in Laos. The local shopkeepers pointed me into the right direction. When I finally found this unassuming roadside cafe, it shone like a beacon to me. It was my link to the rural community's vegan community. They became my friends and an incredible source of information and support. I had a home and could share stories and learn about being vegan in their village. This is a connection I have kept over the years, returning to visit often. As you prepare for your trip, research existing vegan communities you can connect with at your destination.

Having a support system in an unfamiliar place can make it easier to navigate staying vegan while traveling, as well as make the experience all the more enjoyable. When the going gets tough, remember that everyone needs community. Don't lose faith. You've been so strong this far into your personal adventure. Reinforce your beliefs, values, and lifestyle choices with a support group. You can grow your tribe on your travels, forming your global vegan community as you go.

Let's look at the ways to connect and find our tribe:

VOLUNTEER

The most direct way to connect is to get involved with the community and share a common goal. And the most fulfilling way to engage with the local vegan community is to volunteer. Not only will you meet other vegans— you will also have the chance to learn more about local culture, veganism, vegan food production, vegan cooking, farmed animals, and activism.

This is a great way to give back and promote sustainable, eco-friendly practices while connecting with like-minded members of the community. Depending on the role you serve, you may even receive free meals and accommodation for your efforts.

- **WWOOF/HelpX/WorkAway:** These organizations connect travelers with host organizations—usually farm stays, but sometimes non-profit organizations, communes, or families looking for an exchange. This is a great way to connect, learn, and travel on a budget. All three of these organizations charge a subscription, however the price is minimal in comparison to the resources provided. Note that these aren't vegan-based programs, yet there are plenty of vegan opportunities to be found on these platforms! www.wwoofinternational.org / www.helpx.net / www.workaway.info

- **Voluntouring:** Voluntouring.org lists organizations world-wide searching for volunteers. These range from farms and communities to reputable wildlife rescue and rehabilitation centers. There are many companies offering this kind of experience—but remember to always check their credibility. www.voluntouring.org
- **Plant-based Food Pantries:** Plant-based food pantries aren't as popular as WWOOFing farms, however they are on the rise. Search your destination to find out if there are vegan food pantries or food bank gardens you can help out at.
- **Farmed Animal Sanctuaries:** Joining a workday at a farmed animal sanctuary is a great way to give back, remind yourself of why it's important to abstain from consuming animal-derived products, and meet other people with the same interests. Other sanctuary volunteering opportunities involve rescued lab-testing animals, pet shelters, exotic animal rescues, and wildlife rehabilitation centers. A great resource to find sanctuaries at your destination of choice is: www. sanctuaryfederation.org/find-a-sanctuary
- **Other Vegan Organizations:** Search for other vegan organizations, societies, and activist groups and ask about how to get involved!

FIND TRAVEL BUDDIES

*"Surround yourself only with people
who are going to take you higher."*
OPRAH WINFREY

Don't want to travel alone, but can't find anyone to book your trip with? The website "Veg Travel Buddies" connects traveling vegans looking for a travel companion. Enter your travel date and destination, hit search, and connect with others!

Traveling with someone you haven't met before can be intimidating, but is a rewarding and fun experience, so long as you make sure you both want the same things out of your experience and share some common dream-destinations.

You can also use this resource to find a local meeting for coffee, answering your questions about local food options and excursions, or cooking a meal together. Find travel stories, vegan blogs, learn ways to meet locals, and join chat forums.

www.vegtravelbuddies.com

TRAVEL AGENCIES AND TOUR COMPANIES

Don't feel like doing the research and planning yourself? No worries. Whether you want someone to plan an excursion on your trip or plan your full nine-month trek, there is a company out there with the ability to help you book the experience of your dreams. There are tons of options now for vegan tour groups who will organize sightseeing and destination adventures for your entire trip.

Humane Travel and VegVoyages are two reputable touring companies working to reduce the environmental impact of traveling while organizing humane-ensured excursions.

VegVoyages even supplies vegan meals for the duration of the trip.
www.vegantravelasia.com

MEETUP

MeetUp describes themselves as a service used to organize online groups that host in-person and virtual events for people with similar interests. Events can be accessed through both the website and the app. Before setting off, look for a vegan meetup at your destination.

Can't find a group or event? Make your own! It's a creative endeavor that can offer something back to the local community you're visiting. Who knows, maybe they'll keep it going after you leave!
www.meetup.com

VEG VISITS

Need vegan accommodation? Wish your host shared your dietary preferences? Need to find a kitchen space where you don't have to worry if the pots have lingering grease from animal fat?

"VegVisits" is the easiest way to find a vegan-friendly accommodation. You can rent a room or an entire house in over eighty countries worldwide. They offer unique stays as well, such as campgrounds, farm stays, animal sanctuaries, and bungalows. You can even filter your search by kitchen type (vegetarian or vegan) and host diet.

Having a vegetarian host is a great way to help you find the best vegan restaurants, local markets, and attraction destinations within the country. You'll likely meet fellow vegan travelers at the shared destinations, and of course, your host is a direct link to the local vegan community. www.vegvisits.com

SOCIAL MEDIA

It turns out social media can be utilized for more than selfies and political "debates." In fact, it can even be a useful tool if directed more purposefully. Social media is a platform that almost every organization in the world is hooked into. Travelers, vegan and otherwise, have begun to take advantage of this opportunity by sharing their experiences and forming virtual communities.

- **Facebook**: On Facebook, you can search for events, public figures, and groups to help aide your immersion into a foreign vegan scene. A favorite vegan Facebook group of mine is 'Vegan Travel' which hosts a community of over 36,000 vegans who share a love of traveling the globe while continuing to follow their plant-based diets. You can also find groups dedicated to your specific travel locale by searching 'Vegans in (city of choice)'. This will lead you to groups, events, and specific posts referencing this phrase.
  https://www.facebook.com/groups/847126188699892
  https://www.facebook.com/vegantravel

  Come join my vegan family on my Facebook group: **"Brave New Vegan World."**

- **Foodies**: Search Instagram and Google for vegan foodies and reach out to them. On Instagram, use specific hashtags to narrow your search. I know, this sounds crazy intimidating! But the people behind the blogs and vlogs are just that—people.

And in this case, they are highly passionate vegan people. The majority of foodies welcome interactions with other vegans and are happy to answer your questions. Want to know what local food is easiest to veganize? What restaurant serves slow-cooked vegan food made with intent? Ask them! Want to be extra bold? Ask them to join you.

- **Forums:** Forums are online discussion boards, organized by topic. These are great places to throw out your most pressing vegan questions and search for vegan travel advice. www. Veganforum.org is a useful resource for this and has many threads on vegan travel, some of which even give great detail on specific destinations. This is a can't-miss resource when researching your destination of choice.

COUCHSURFING

Traveling on a budget? Couchsurfing is another resource for finding a place to stay—in this case a free place to stay. Couchsurfing is exactly what it sounds like—traveling the world one couch at a time. (Ironically, most Couchsurfing hosts offer surfers a proper bed for their stay.) Hosts benefit by getting to meet interesting people from a variety of ethnicities and backgrounds, and travelers benefit by getting a place to crash and a local to get the scoop from. This is a fun and adventurous way to meet people while stretching your travel budget further.

The app isn't intended for finding vegan hosts, yet it can be done. You can search for vegan hosts, or read the profiles of others traveling in the same area as you to see if any are vegan too. Couchsurfing allows users to create and attend events, and some fortuitously happen to be vegan potlucks! www.couchsurfing.com

VEGAN ACTIVITIES

Have fun while you meet people by joining a vegan-centered activity. Attending a class, workshop, or presentation is a great way to meet like-minded people. This can be one of the easiest ways to put yourself out there, especially if you're traveling solo. Many times, the leaders of these activities will find ways to get the group talking to each other and engaged. Even if they don't, you have common ground to get you started. Be brave, and make the first move!

As a disclosure, none of the following companies are vegan based. You need to do your diligence to make sure the plant-based experience is vegan to your definition. Contact the host ahead of time to discuss your needs and expectations.

- **TripAdvisor:** TripAdvisor helps users find more than flights and hotels. Check out their 'Things to do' tab for a listing of popular activities, museums, and eateries. You can use that resource to search for vegan activities in the area you will be visiting. **www.tripadvisor.com**

- **AirBnB Experiences:** The 'Experiences' section of AirBnB lists one-of-a-kind activities hosted by experts. Cooking classes, book talks, food tours, local outings, and much more can be found here. Join a vegan cooking class or attend a gardening workshop to learn a new skill while immersing in the local plant-based community. Many times, these experiences have an even blend of locals and travelers attending, giving you a wide breadth of people to engage with. Worst case scenario, you get your hands in the dirt and a plate of yummy food. **www.airbnb.com/experiences**

- **Groupon:** Groupon is a website that's been here through the ages of the internet. They offer discounts on local services, restaurants, classes, and experiences. Pair this up with your TripAdvisor finds to save some money. **www.groupon.com**

REBEL VEGAN TOP TIP:

Use Groupon and other saver-websites to find a coupon for a buy-one-get-one-free vegan lunch or activity. Use this as an excuse to invite a new friend out for the afternoon!

VEGAN EVENTS

"You have to find a tribe."
RUPAUL

Want to throw your hands up, dance to the music, and get down on some food-truck falafel bites?

Attending a vegan event is the most exciting way to introduce yourself to the vegan community. More international, national, regional, and even traveling vegan events are popping up year by year. These range from conferences with informational and inspirational speakers, to food-based events where attendees can try an assortment of vegan dishes, to three-day camp-out music festivals.

www.VegEvents.com connects people with vegan events worldwide and provides resources to event organizers. Additionally, a listing of vegan festivals around the globe can be found in the resources section of this guide.

Can't find anything or need more community? Don't worry - there's one last ditch effort. Start talking! Technology is great and offers us a ton of resources for finding people and opportunities we otherwise likely wouldn't.

Take advantage of the fact that you have this resource available to you, but don't stop there. Don't be afraid to fall back on the tried-and-true tactic of talking to people. If your GPS malfunctioned, you wouldn't think twice about asking for directions. If you're lost in your vegan journey, don't be ashamed to ask someone to point you in the right direction.

When you come across a vegan restaurant, event, or even a health-food store chat up the workers and the patrons to find out more. These are the richest sources of information for the local vegan scene.

THE MAN WHO FORGOT TO DIE[5]

In 1976, Stamatis Moraitis was given a diagnosis nobody ever wants: he had advanced lung cancer. His doctor said he had six to nine months to live. He considered for a moment staying in the US and pursuing aggressive cancer treatment, but high medical and funeral costs motivated him to make a different decision - he would return to his home, the Greek island of Ikaria. This way, his wife Elpiniki could use his retirement savings.

Stamatis and his wife moved into a tiny whitewashed house set in two acres of vineyards. At first, Stamatis kept to his bed. Then childhood friends learned of his return and started showing up every afternoon for long chats over a bottle or two of wine. "I might as well die happy," thought Stamatis. But instead of deteriorating as the doctors had predicted, Stamatis felt stronger. He began to plant vegetables, thinking at least his wife could enjoy them when he was gone.

Six months came and went. Stamatis did not die. He carried on planting his garden, and eased himself into the island routine - getting up when the sunrise woke him, working in the vineyard until mid-afternoon, lunching on plant-based foods, taking a nap, then spending the evening at the local tavern, playing dominoes and enjoying two or three cups of local wine a day.

What happened to the cancer? "It just went away," said Stamatis. I went back to America about 25 years after moving here to see if the doctors could explain it to me. My doctors were all dead."

Stamatis died peacefully of old age in his island home, in 2013. He was 102 years old.

The remote island of Ikaria is off the coast of Turkey, home to around 10,000 people. On this island, people live on average ten years longer than people in the rest of Europe and America. There are fewer rates of cancer, chronic disease, depression and dementia. What's more, they maintain a sex life into old age and stay active well into their 90's. The secret to Ikarians' longevity and healthy life? Their diet and lifestyle. A relaxed pace that ignores the clock while focusing on community, and a diet high in vegetables, greens, herbs, beans and potatoes, with minimal meat or refined sugar.

Ikaria is one of the world's Blue Zones - these are areas where inhabitants live longer, healthier lives than anywhere else. What these areas have in common is that their populations eat a diet made up of whole, plant-based foods, with minimal meat and dairy... By going plant-based, you are taking a leaf out of their book and setting yourself up for a long, vibrant life!

BLUE
ZONES

Blue zones are regions where a higher than usual number of people live much longer than average.
There are five blue zone areas in the world.

LOMA LINDA
UNITED STATES

NICOYA
COSTA RICA

SARDINIA
ITALY

ICARIA
GREECE

OKINAWA
JAPAN

8

BUMPS IN THE ROAD[1]

"I have no illusions. I lost them in my travels."
VICOMTE DE VALMONT IN DANGEROUS LIASONS

Travel is very humbling as our lives and worries are put in proportion; you realize what a tiny place you occupy in the world. I believe this process is liberating and gives us a fresh perspective or lens in which we can overcome any future dilemmas. But it is important to recognize and prepare for the basic fact: Bumps in the road will happen—in life, in veganism, and in travel.

Setting out on an adventure can be intimidating, especially when trying to do so while adhering to a certain lifestyle. But remember that veganism shouldn't be restrictive; it can open up your world with the right attitude and know-how. Not every moment of your journey is going to be perfect, or ideal, or even what you thought it was going to be.

Trust me when I say I have experienced my own fair share of bumps, roadblocks, detours, and smoking engines. It's important to recognize that these obstacles are on the road ahead. Instead of looking at these hiccups as something stopping you, try viewing them as something pushing you to be better. Because at the end of the day, that's what they are doing.

What matters is how you react, recover, adapt, and move forward. Try to get some perspective and not overreact. Ultimately, it will all become anecdotes or travel stories that you laugh about one day when back home. They will end up making you nostalgic for travel and adventure—for those times you lived life on the edge.

The beauty of travel is that it takes you out of your element. It's an opportunity to put yourself out there, try new things, achieve personal triumphs, and push yourself to be the best version of you. Looking back, I see that the bumps I've overcome in my road are what pushed me to grow and to learn the most. The difficulties opened my eyes. The bad days made me humble, and the good days taught me to be grateful.

Ultimately, a bad day on the road is still a day of freedom on the open road! What's important is to stay positive, and remember everything you've accomplished and overcome in your journey so far. Even buying your ticket and packing your bag shows bravery, ambition, and a will to drive you forward.

> *"Travel is fatal to prejudice, bigotry,*
> *and narrow-mindedness."*
> **MARK TWAIN**

There are three key lessons I've learned when it comes to overcoming obstacles.

1. The first is to be flexible. When traveling, not everything is going to go according to plan. You might find that you've accidentally been served something with butter in it, or you may be offered a local delicacy during one of your excursions. Be open to facing these challenges. Have an idea of how you would like to handle these situations in mind, but be able to tackle each hurdle as it comes.

2. The second lesson I've learned is the importance of having an open mind and heart when traveling. It's important to connect when attempting to learn and respect a new culture. An advantage of this is that building ties with the locals can be the easiest way to get yourself out of hot water. Having someone to turn to with local knowledge and access to services has saved me a number of times. Showing that you respect local customs and care about a community and their home will give them a reason to care about you. Don't be afraid to tap into this rich resource.

3. The third lesson is to be prepared. While you can't predict what is going to happen out there, you can think about it and make an educated guess. The easiest way to remain calm during turbulent times is to not be caught off guard.

To help get you started, I'd like to touch on some of the most common struggles people face while abroad, and share what I've found helps to prepare for and overcome difficulties, such as cultural and language barriers, difficulties finding vegan food, accidentally eating non-vegan foods, and traveling with a non-vegan companion.

LANGUAGE BARRIERS

The first bump in the road is the most common, and the easiest to overcome. Not being able to speak the same language as the majority of the people in the country you're visiting can be extremely frustrating at times. Simple things like ordering dinner, asking for a bathroom, getting directions, and making a friend become exponentially more difficult.

Luckily, you already know what to do! Use your food cards and your translating apps to help get you through. If you're feeling ambitious, you can even download a language learning app and master the basics of the language. With the basics down, you'll be surprised how quickly you start to catch on once immersed in the language.

No time to learn the language before going? Don't fret. You can always make a bilingual friend along the way to help you out.

CULTURAL BARRIERS

In some regions, you may be the first vegetarian or vegan that people might have met, and they may not understand what you need from them. Some destinations won't even have specific words for being vegan. Be ready to explain yourself in greater detail than you're used to doing back home. It's helpful to be able to explain the 'what' and the 'why' clearly and in a kind manner.

It's common to tell someone you are vegan, only to be handed a non-vegan dish or an improperly veganized dish, such as a cup of brothy soup with the chunks of meat picked out. This scenario can take tact to navigate, as in some cultures it's rude to deny an offered meal. A great way to prevent this is to offer to help cook when staying with host families. This allows you to see what's going into the food and respectfully interject before it's too late.

If you do get offered a dish you can't eat, it's up to you how you want to handle it. Take some time before setting off to think about how you would like to handle this scenario. Would you rather adapt to local customs and eat the dish, or explain that you hold the value of not eating animals too strongly and respectfully refuse? Both scenarios are acceptable, and only you can decide which is right for you.

A cultural barrier that you don't get a say in is the treatment and display of cruel animal welfare. Many regions of the world have different perspectives of animals than we do, from looking at animals as a whole to looking at them on a species-by-species basis. You might see starving stray cats and dogs, a carcass hung in front of a butcher shop, an animal we would view as a pet kenneled at a soup kitchen, or public abuse and misuse of farm animals. It's unfair that these things happen in the world. But you must accept that you will see it.

Only you can decide what standards of animal welfare you can accept in a travel destination. Let's face it, the standards of animal welfare at home aren't perfect either. Steady and mentally prepare yourself for this one, but don't stop yourself because of it. Simply don't participate. Go out and spread the word, fight the good fight, and use what you see out there to reinforce your vegan ideals. If you can't shake the things you encounter, then use that as fuel to act. Donate, volunteer, and speak out to make a difference.

> *"Travel isn't always pretty. It isn't always comfortable. Sometimes it hurts, it even breaks your heart. But that's okay. The journey changes you; it should change you. It leaves marks on your memory, on your consciousness, on your heart, and on your body. You take something with you. Hopefully, you leave something good behind."*
> **ANTHONY BOURDAIN**

STAYING NOURISHED

Some locations make it easier than others to find the food you need as a vegan. Every once in a while, you will come across a town where it seems the restaurants have nothing for you to eat. At the same time, the markets may be sparse on produce, and definitely lacking on anything tofu related.

I've found that even when a town *seems* like it won't have anything vegan to offer, I can usually find a plate in at least one establishment. Research the local food to see what dishes are usually vegan or can easily be veganized, and utilize helpful food finder applications like HappyCow, Yelp, and TripAdvisor.

Still no luck? Don't worry. There is always something to be whipped up at even the sparsest of grocery stores. Tortillas, salsa, and beans make a protein-rich tostada. Bread, jam, and fruit make a quick sandwich. Just be sure to have the names and spelling of common ingredients to avoid (eggs, dairy, butter, cream, meat broths) saved on a notecard or in your phone to make your shopping experience go smoother.

MAKING MISTAKES

Unfortunately, many vegans have experienced that heart-sinking moment where they realize they have just accidentally eaten something containing animal products. This moment can feel terrible, I know from experience. Try to stay calm and remember that it was an accident, and that you are doing the best that you can.

To help prevent this from happening, ask questions. Use your food cards and do your best to ensure that the dish you will receive is 100% vegan. Personally, when unsure, I choose something else.

But sometimes, even after triple-checking, you find out you still made a mistake. In these cases, it can be tempting to be angry at the establishment, host, or cook. Most times, the non-vegan dish wasn't intentionally served to us. Many people in the world don't understand what veganism is, and language barriers further complicate this. Use this as an opportunity to share and inform people about this aspect of your lifestyle.

If done sensitively, it is one of the kindest things you can do, as it inspires them to become aware and improve their diets. You may even save lives. And of course, tuck this lesson away to try to steer away from repeating it in the future.

A bump in the road can wake us up, refocus us, and make us feel alive. I always say that veganism, like life, is about the journey...not the destination. Learn from the bumps in the road and enjoy the ride. Above all, don't let fear get the best of you. It's important to remember that the ethos of the Rebel Vegan traveler is to go out there and "risk the bad meal" in hopes of getting the good one.

Be compassionate with yourself, and remember that it's okay if you aren't able to be perfect with your eating. Connect, share your story, and take something away from the journey. If you can do that, you've had a good trip, no matter what bumps you've encountered along the way.

Remember that these bumps will become great stories, the stories you'll tell to your grandchildren, part of what makes you you. It is not the end of the journey but rather lessons to help you live your best life!

9

FINAL DESTINATION
THE GARDEN OF VEGAN

"I can't change the direction of the wind, but I can adjust my sails to always reach my destination."
JIMMY DEAN[1]

This may be the closing chapter and final destination of our journey here, but it is only the beginning of a lifetime of vegan adventures for you, my fellow rebels. I am excited for you and hope our time together has helped to inspire, demystify, and uncomplicate vegan travel.

At its essence, traveling is about the sense of freedom that comes from teetering into the new. That unrivaled, dizzying feeling of living on the edge. That gorgeous sensation of discovery; of literally flying into the unknown.

And veganism—like travel—is a lifelong journey of discovery. There is always more to explore, learn, taste. And, by combining the two, you align your values and passions to present the best version of yourself to the world.

REBEL VEGANS—and that's you by the way—are trailblazers. We have rejected the old ways and status quo and are building a better world. Traveling and connecting is a big part of that. By wandering outside of the big cities and our comfort zones, we will encounter challenges and opportunities to connect in new ways. Our travels together through this book will leave you ready to go out and embrace the world as your authentic self. This honestly and compassion will translate in every language and be the key to opening up the world. You are part of a movement and helping to put veganism on the map.

As promised, an extensive resource section listing all the websites, apps, and other resources mentioned in the guidebook is waiting for you on the next pages.

I've also thrown in some extra resources, including my recommended reading list of vegan classics, to keep you entertained on those long journeys or lounging poolside. Before the resource section, you'll find my rebel recipes for the road. These quick and easy recipes are kept simple, adaptable, and can be made almost anywhere. They have been road-tested with love!

If you haven't read the first two books in the Rebel Vegan series, I recommend checking them out. *REBEL VEGAN LIFE: A Radical Take on Veganism for a Brave New World*, is the first post-Covid analysis of why veganism matters in this new era. It's a deep thinkers guide to the vegan movement. Its follow-up companion book, *REBEL VEGAN LIFE: A Plant-Based Nutrition & Beginner's Guide*, is more a nuts & bolts exploration and practical resource on how to incorporate veganism into your daily life and build sustainable habits for your best life.

For now, it's time to say goodbye, my fellow rebels. Thank you for believing in *REBEL VEGAN* and opening yourself up to new ideas, places, and connections. It was an honor to share the journey, and I wish you safe travels in this brave new world.

London Todd Sinclair

10

VEGAN TRAVEL RECIPES[1]

"The Gods created certain kinds of beings to replenish our bodies; they are the trees and the plants and the seeds."

PLATO

"My body will not be a tomb for other creatures."

LEONARDO DA VINCI

Welcome to our *REBEL VEGAN* Recipe section!

Life on the road is deliciously unpredictable, so we chose to create 16 simple, healthy, and satiating meals that can be adjusted depending on the fresh produce, legumes, or grains that you find throughout your trip.

Some of the recipes can be prepared before you head off, such as the stuffed dates, energy balls, and the trail mix—those are great to bring on longer flights or journeys where vegan options may be limited.

The seed mix and the Muesli can also be stored in containers or zip bags, so you won't even have to think of what to have for breakfast the first days in a new environment. A specific corner of my suitcase stores a Tupperware container with my Muesli. Then I buy plant-based milk at a local shop on arrival. This way, my mornings in an unknown location are relaxed and at my own pace.

All the recipes are easy to recreate and versatile, so play around with the ingredients and have fun!!

USEFUL TOOLS TO BRING ONTO YOUR TRIP:

- Wooden Spoon and Fork
- Jackknife
- Nut Bag – these are great if you cannot seem to find a place that sells plant milk
- Zip Bags and/or Containers – perfect to store leftover food in
- Can Opener
- Reusable Water Bottle
- Rubber Bands

REBEL VEGAN'S COFFEE MAKER SOUP HACK

It's a simple and cheap meal if you want to relax in your hotel room. And canned soups are surprisingly healthy. Grab some local bread to dip in it, and you've got a whole meal—and a night in!

(You do need to ensure that your hotel room has a classic hotplate coffee maker)

- **Bring or buy a can of your favorite vegan soup. Almost every corner shop in the world seems to stock canned soup.**
- **Turn on the coffee maker stand (do not add water to the filter).**
- **Open and pour your soup into the coffee pot.**
- **Put the pot on the hot plate and wait for it to heat your soup.**
- **Serve in one of the hotel room's coffee mugs.**

OPTIONAL: Buy some local bread

And Presto!

After a long day of sightseeing, you have a lovely warm meal in the privacy of your own hotel room.

Trail Mix

**SERVES
1**

Ingredients

**2 or 3 different types of
dried fruits (e.g. fig, apricot,
cranberries)**

**2 or 3 different types of nuts
(e.g. walnuts, Brazil nuts,
pistachios)**

Optional: shaved coconut

Directions

- This recipe is rather simple, but a great inspiration for you to play around with along your trip.

- Simply bring a light container or zip bag (or prepare in advance) and mix together any kind of dried fruits and nuts.

- I find it helpful to sometimes cut the fruits and nuts into smaller pieces, especially if they only come in bigger shapes.

- That's obviously up to you, though, and won't change the quality of the final product!

- If you store the mix in an air-tight and dry, cold place, it keeps for a long time.

You can prepare this recipe before you head off!

That way, you'll have something nourishing to bring along the trip!

Seeds Mix

SERVES 1

Ingredients

Pumpkin Seeds
Sunflower Seeds
(chopped) Cashews
Sesame
Sea Salt

Directions

- Mix together equal amounts of pumpkin and sunflower seeds.
- Add in half of that amount of chopped cashew nuts, and a few tablespoons of sesame seeds.
- Mix together with a bit of salt and keep in an air-tight container/bag in a cold and dark place.

This is great to prepare in advance and keep with you along the trip, as it's a great topping for almost any type of dish!

Energy Balls

**SERVES
1**

Ingredients

8 (Medjool) Dates

~3/4 - 1 cup (250ml) Walnuts

~ ¼ cup (60ml) unsweetened Cacao

Optional: dash of Cinnamon

Sesame and cacao for decoration

Directions

- If you're using dates that are not pitted, remove the stone before adding all of the listed ingredients in a high speed food processor.

- Roll the dough into equally sized balls and cover with sesame/cacao.

- Store in a dark and cold place!

Smoothie Bowl

**SERVES
1**

Ingredients

1 (frozen) banana

~1 cup (frozen) berries

Dash of plant milk

Optional: sweetener of choice

+ whatever suitable and delicious toppings you may find

Directions

- Blend everything together in a blender and pour into a serving bowl.

- Garnish with whatever delicious toppings you can find in your area.

DIY Granola / Muesli

**SERVES
1**

Ingredients

2.5 cups rolled oats

¼ cup maple syrup

1 ½ tsp cinnamon

½ tsp nutmeg

1 tbsp vanilla extract

3 tbsp coconut oil

2 tbsp nut butter (e.g. almond)

1/2 cup almonds, chopped or sliced

2 tbsp sesame seeds

Pinch of Salt

Directions

- Preheat your oven to about 180 dg.C. or 350 dg.F. .
- In a large mixing bowl, bring together all the ingredients listed, except the nuts.
- Spread on a baking tray lined with a sheet of baking paper, and transfer to the oven for about 25 to 35 minutes (depending on where you are located and what type of oven you're using).
- Make sure to mix around every 5 to 10 minutes to avoid burning.
- After about 10 to 15 minutes, add in your nuts and seeds and wait until the whole mix
- looks slightly golden brown.

Store in a dark and cold place.

Stuffed Dates

SERVES 1

Ingredients

Medjool Dates

Nut Butter (e.g. cashew or peanut)

Chia Seeds

Nuts (e.g. walnuts)

Directions

You can prepare this recipe before you head off!

That way, you'll have something nourishing to bring along the trip!

- If you can only find dates that haven't been pitted, make sure to cut them open on one side and remove the stone.
- Press some nut butter into the date, and add whatever type of nut you can find and like.
- Cover the open side with some chia seeds – done!

- Store in a dark and cold place.

Poke Bowl

**SERVES
1**

Ingredients

2 handful fresh leafy greens
¼ medium size cucumber
Small handful grapes
½ - 1 small sweet potato
Pomegranate seeds
Optional: Trail mix

Dressing

2-3 tsp mustard
1 tbsp sweetener of choice
1/3 cup oil (e.g. olive, if possible)
2 tbsp vinegar
Touch of garlic powder
Salt and Pepper to taste

Directions

- Cut your sweet potato into bite-size pieces and cook in salted water.
- In the meantime, prepare the rest of the bowl.
- Wash your greens and put them on the bottom of your bowl.
- Slice some grapes in half and add onto the greens, together with some freshly cut up cucumber and a few pomegranate seeds.
- Add your cooked sweet potato to the bowl and drizzle the mustard dressing all over.
- Finish off with some of our previously prepared trail mix.

SERVES 1

RAW Avocado Choco Pudding

Ingredients

1 ripe avocado

1.5 – 2 tbsp unsweetened cacao powder

3 – 4 tsp sweetener of choice (e.g. maple syrup)

50 – 60ml / 1.5 – 2 fl oz plant milk (e.g. almond)

Optional: Vanilla extract

Directions

- Blend everything together and enjoy right away!

Corn Bowl

**SERVES
1**

Ingredients

**2 to 4 tbsp lentils + three
times the amount of water**

**½ portion rice (according to
package)**

1 small white onion

1 clove of garlic

1 ½ tsp caraway

**1 tbsp (sunflower or
rapeseed) oil**

**1 tbsp smoked paprika
powder**

Fresh Spinach

Salt and Pepper to taste

Oil

½ Lime

Tahini Dressing

2 tbsp tahini

Juice of 1/3 lemon or lime

½ tsp sweetener of choice

Salt and Pepper to taste

Directions

- Start by adding a little oil to a pan over medium heat, and mix in all the spices.
- Chop up onion and garlic and sauté until translucent and covered in spices.
- Pour in lentils and water, and cook until soft.
- Simultaneously cook some rice and wash your spinach.
- In a small mixing bowl, mix together all the ingredients for the dressing and set aside.
- Assemble your bowl and drizzle over the dressing!

Tomato Soup

**SERVES
3-4**

Ingredients

850g/ 300 oz tomatoes

2 small white onions

2 garlic cloves

3 tbsp vegetable broth

4 tbsp tomato paste

~600/ 20 fl oz ml water

Dried oregano

Olive oil

Salt and Pepper to taste

Directions

- Chop the onion into small pieces and mince the garlic. Add both to a cooking pot with some olive oil, and sauté over medium heat until translucent.

- Add all the spices and mix together, before chopping the tomatoes into small cubes and adding them to the pot.

- Pour in your vegetable broth (water + vegetable stock) and let everything cook down until the tomatoes have fully fallen apart.

- Blend and serve immediately.

Note: *If you don't have a blender, use canned tomato soup and simply sauté garlic and onion in olive oil before adding in the soup.*

Coconut – Bean Soup

**SERVES
3-4**

Ingredients

1 can white beans

1 can coconut milk

2 tsp lime juice

Few slices of ginger

2 cloves garlic

1 beet root

1 medium sized carrot

Salt and (white) Pepper to taste

Directions

- Mince the garlic and add to a cooking pot with some oil.
- Cook over medium heat until translucent, then add in the slices of (peeled) ginger.
- Add in a can of white beans and a can of coconut milk.
- Let cook until the beans seem really soft, then blend together in a blender.
- If you don't happen to find one, make sure to cut the ginger into small pieces and enjoy the soup as is.
- Season with some salt and pepper, and add some freshly shredded or thinly sliced vegetables on top.

SERVES 2-3

Green Peas Rice

Ingredients

~ 1 Portion of rice (according to package)

130g/4.5 oz frozen green peas

1 small bell pepper

1 small white onion

2 cloves garlic

1 tbsp smoked paprika powder

Vegetable Broth

Cilantro

Lemon / Lime

Salt and Pepper to taste

Directions

- In a small pot, cook one portion of rice, adding some vegetable broth to the water.

- In the meantime, mince the garlic and chop onion and bell pepper into small cubes.

- Throw everything in a greased cooking pan and sauté over low-medium heat.

- Once translucent, mix in your peas.

- *If you're using fresh peas for this, please add water to the pan to cook them down, otherwise they will remain too hard inside, while the rest is almost cooked through already.*

- Season with smoked paprika, salt, and pepper, and serve with freshly chopped cilantro and lime juice!

Lentil Dahl

**SERVES
2-4**

Ingredients

2 cups lentils (red or brown)

~7 cups water

1 medium size white onion

2 – 3 cloves garlic

Oil

2,5 tbsp tomato paste

2 tsp mustard seeds

1,5 tbsp paprika powder

1 tsp turmeric powder

1 tsp ground coriander

Juice of 1/3 lemon

Directions

- Sauté sliced onion and garlic in a pan with some oil over medium heat.

- Add all the condiments and tomato paste to the pan, followed by lentils, and pour in enough water to fully cover the lentils.

- Cover with a lid and cook down until soft.

- Enjoy with some fresh coriander and lemon juice!

SERVES 2

Mashed Potatoes with Gravy and Shredded Vegetables

Ingredients

~750g / 25 oz potatoes + 1 small potato

~175g/ 6 oz Brown button mushrooms

~120g/ 4 oz Cauliflower

1 medium white onion

Vegetable Broth / Salt and Pepper to taste

1 beet root

1 large carrot

Optional: fresh greens e.g. parsley

Directions

- Start off by peeling your potatoes and cooking them in a pot until soft (you can already
- add salt to the water in this step, or simply season while mashing).
- In a separate pot, cook the mushrooms and chopped up cauliflower in some vegetable
- broth or salt and pepper in case you can not find any.
- Rinse the mix, saving about 75 ml/ 2 to 3 fl oz of the broth to either blend or mash
- mushrooms and cauliflower in.
- Rinse and drain the potatoes, then mash them together with some olive oil if possible.
- If you didn't cook them in salted water, just season them now.
- Shred up some fresh vegetables like beet root and carrot to go on top.

Sweet Potato Stir Fry

**SERVES
2**

Ingredients

250g / 8.5 oz Cauliflower

**200g / 7 oz carrots or 2
medium size carrots**

1⁄2 Medium size sweet potato

Red bell pepper

**130g / 4.5 oz Mushrooms or
about 10 small-medium size**

2 Cloves of garlic

2-3 tbsp Spring onion

Oil

**Optional: chilies, fresh lime
juice**

Directions

- Cut the sweet potato into small cubes and throw into a pan with some oil and finely minced garlic.

- Fry for about a minute, then add enough water to almost cover the sweet potato.

- Let cook over high heat for about 5 minutes with a lid on.

- Chop up the cauliflower and carrots and throw into the pan, reducing the heat to medium heat.

- Cut the mushrooms and add them to the pan before you season with salt, black pepper, and paprika spice.

- You can mix in some chilies and spring onion, too!

**SERVES
2**

Wraps / Burritos

Ingredients

Small portion of Quinoa or
Rice

~ ½ can kidney beans

6 small tomatoes

½ medium size carrot

2 cloves garlic

Juice of ½ lime

½ medium size white onion

Fresh coriander

2 tbsp tomato paste

Oil

Salt and pepper to taste

Wraps / Tortillas

Lettuce

Optional: Vegan Mayo

Directions

• Start by mincing 1 clove of garlic and about ¼ white onion, and add them to a pan with oil over medium heat.

• Add in the quinoa and cook in some salted water or vegetable broth.

• Mix in about 2 tablespoons of tomato paste (if accessible) and some dried herbs.

• Once almost fully cooked, rinse and drain the beans and stir them into the mix.

• Cover with a lid and let cook until done. Set aside.

• To prepare the salsa, either shred or chop up some carrot, the tomatoes, rest of the onion, the other garlic clove and whisk it together in a small bowl with some lime juice and oil.

• Season with salt and pepper as well as some freshly chopped coriander.

Assemble your wraps and enjoy!

11

RESOURCES

In my years of veganism and travel, I have collected a treasure trove of resources to help me along my way. I've done my best to share this knowledge and information with you in my Rebel Vegan series. To help you quickly access this information while on the go, I have compiled all of the resources mentioned in this guide into one compact resource section. Feel free to dog-ear these pages and references when needed in your life and adventures.

WEBSITES

Save these websites to your Favorites Bar before preparing your next vegan vacation. These resources will make the planning process considerably easier.

- **Plant Based Health Online**: The top plant-based doctors in the UK offering healthcare and lifestyle advice to overcome chronic illnesses and certain cancers. *PlantBasedHealthOnline.com*

- **Plant Based Healthcare Professionals**: This patient/ public resources are incredible with factsheets, news roundups and webinars etc on healthy plant-based diets. *PlantBasedHealthProfessionals.com/factsheets*

- **Vegan Fitness**: This is a UK based community with discusses everything vegan and fitness related. Their forums cover all aspects of a vegan lifestyle with an emphasis on sports training, health, and fitness. You can answer all your questions here! *www.veganfitness.net/*

- **HappyCow**: This website is helpful for finding vegan restaurants around the world. It is user-sourced, so you can add or update restaurants, as well as read customer reviews. Bonus, this website comes in app form too. *HappyCow.net*

- **VegVisits**: The Airbnb for vegans. Book unique homestays and accommodations with locals in over 80 countries. *VegVisits.com*

- **Vegan Meetups, Couchsurfing, and Traveling**: A Facebook community with 7,000 members. Vegan gatherings and open Couchsurfing opportunities are listed here. Members also discuss travel experiences and questions. You have to request membership for this group. *facebook.com/groups/974772789309783*

- **Barnivore**: A searchable directory of wines, beers, and liquors denoting which are vegan-friendly. *barnivore.com*

- **Vegan Travel Facebook Group**: The group currently has over 35,000 members. The content discusses all things vegan related, and many members are more than happy to answer your questions. *facebook.com/groups/vegantravel*

- **Vegan Travel**: Virtual vegan community with reviews, blog posts, videos, and more for planning your vegan trips. *VeganTravel.com*

- **Foundation for Intentional Community**: Want to live with other vegans? Interested in growing your own food? How about popping in for a weekend visit? Use this website to access a global directory of intentional communities. The advanced search option lets users narrow the search to vegetarian and/or vegan communities. *ic.org*

- **Food Labels Exposed**: Use this website put together by A Greener World to help you navigate the confusing world of food labels. *aGreenerWorld.org/wp-content/uploads/2015/03/AGW-Food-Labels-Exposed-2017-EMAIL-SCREEN-8-31-2017.pdf*

- **Animal Welfare's Consumer's Guide**: The Animal Welfare Institute has put together a listing of all food labels and what they mean, explaining which are legal terms and which are made up by the food companies. *awiOnline.org/content/consumers-guide-food-labels-and-animal-welfare*

- **Vegan Calculator**: Ever wished you could measure the impact you've made in your vegan or vegetarian journey? Now you can. Measure your impact at: *VeganCalculator.com*

- **Book Different**: This website rates hotels in terms of their eco-friendliness. *BookDifferent.com*

APPS

Download these apps on your phone ASAP! These resources will help you with just about everything - booking a hotel room, scoring a yummy vegan meal, communicating in a foreign language, and more.

- **Vegan Passport**: This is a digital food card available in various languages to help you explain your dietary preferences. The passport explains in detail which ingredients vegans do and don't eat in 78 different languages.

- **Google Translate**: You can speak or type words and phrases to be translated into over 100 languages. You can even point your camera at a block of text and have it translated for you in real-time. Be sure to download the language pack for the specific language you need, so that the app can be used offline as well.

- **AirVegan**: Use this app when heading to the airport. AirVegan shows how vegan-friendly an airport is. It lists all places that offer vegan options, and even tells you where they are located. Some of you may have encountered this app back when they only supported airports in the United States. Good news - the app went international with its listings back in 2018.

- **Food Monster**: This app provides the user with a database containing over 8,000 vegan recipes. While it isn't travel-related, it can aid you in your travels by providing quick and budget-friendly meals when you select the filters 'Less Than Five Ingredients' or 'Quick Meals'.

- **VeganXpress**: This app only works for travel in the US. It lists all vegan menu choices at 150 chain restaurants throughout the US. The database goes into great detail about all the possible vegan options. It also includes a food guide for supermarkets, and another guide for various alcoholic drinks.

- **V-Cards**: Vegan Abroad: V-cards, vegan cards in this case, are translation cards to help you order food abroad. This is a similar concept to the food cards offered up in the Hot Spots chapter of this guide, only they offer translations in over 100 languages on demand.

- **Veganagogo**: This is another translation app - because you can never have too many. Users choose from a list of pre-written questions and statements, making it easier to use than Google Translate in some scenarios.

- **Foodsaurus**: Standing in the grocery aisle at a foreign market completely unsure of what the ingredient list on the pre-made boxed meal lists? Whip out your phone and scan the ingredient list with Foodsaurus, and the app will translate the label to your language of choice.

- **Veggly**: Can't imagine dating an omnivore? Looking for a romantic partner that can hold you accountable in your vegan journey? Check out Veggly, a vegan dating app currently available in 181 countries.

- **Vegan Check**: This app double checks that products are entirely vegan before purchasing. It also includes services such as tattoo studios and salons.

- **Vegan Pocket**: Vegan Pocket scans barcodes to check if the product is vegan. No more reading confusing food labels! Just scan, and done.

- **abillion | Impact made easy**: This app lets you search for vegan brands and products near you, wherever you are around the world. After finding a vegan product on the app, you can even read customer reviews.

VOLUNTEERING

Want to get involved? Use these websites to find volunteer opportunities in the vegan community.

- **WWOOF**: Worldwide opportunities to volunteer on organic farms. Typically, room and board are offered in exchange. You must create an account for each country you would like to search for hosts in, and a subscription fee is required. *wwoof. net*

- **WorkAway**: Worldwide opportunities to volunteer at organic and non-organic farms, homesteads, communities, non-profit organizations, and more. Room and board are typically offered in exchange. Sometimes hosts offer an hourly wage in addition to this. A small subscription fee is required. *WorkAway.info*

- **HelpX**: HelpX is the same concept as WorkAway (above), without the opportunity for an hourly wage. Room and board are usually offered, and a small subscription fee is required. *helpx.net*

- **Voluntouring**: This blog keeps an up-to-date listing of organizations looking for volunteers. The listing has a tab for listings that strictly adhere to vegan principles. *voluntouring.org*

- **International Volunteering**: Facebook group listing international vegan-based volunteer opportunities. *facebook.com/groups/217244375670902*

- **Grassroots Volunteering**: Database of international grassroots volunteer experiences. Search the site for vegan-centered opportunities, or contact hosts to see if vegans can be accommodated. *GrassRootsVolunteering.org*

- **WorldPackers**: Volunteer experiences and programs for travelers in over 100 countries. *WorldPackers.com*

VEGAN TOURS

These vegan tour guides and agencies take the work and planning out of your adventure, leaving nothing but fun and delicious plant-based food for you. Each has detailed websites listing all of their services and destinations! Even if you don't plan on booking with an agency, they are worth looking at for inspiration and ideas.

P.S. These are tour groups offering international opportunities. If you already have a destination in mind, do a quick Google search for vegan tour guides there. I bet you'll find even more resources!

- **Vegan Food Tours**: European Vegan City Tours.
  VeganFoodTours.com
- **Vegan Adventure Tours**: Specializing in epic tours through Latin American and UK micro tours.
  VeganAdventureHolidays.com
- **Intrepid Travel**: International tour company does several vegan tours annually.
  IntrepidTravel.com/vegan-food-adventures
- **The Nomadic Vegan**: Website for Vegan Tours, Vegan Cruise, and Vegan-friendly tour operators.
  TheNomadicVegan.com/vegan-tours

FESTS AND EVENTS

A great way to have fun and immerse in the vegan culture while traveling is to attend a festival or event. Below I list a number of resources for finding events in several destinations. This list is not exhaustive! Reference it, and then do further research to find even more fun items to add to your travel calendar.

- **Vegan Festivals Directory:** *vegan.com/blog/festivals*
- **VegEvents International:** *VegEvents.com*
- **International Listing:** *vegan.com/blog/festivals*
- **Vegan Society International Listings:** *VeganSociety.com/whats-new/events*
- **HappyCow International Listings:** *HappyCow.net/events*
- **UK Vegan Events:** *VeganEventsUK.co.uk*
- **USA Vegan Events:** *AmericanVegan.org/vegfests*
- **Australia Vegan Events:** *VeganAustralia.org.au/events*

FILMS:

- Cowspiracy (Netflix)
- Seaspiracy (Netflix)
- Earthlings (Free stream on http://www.nationearth.com/)
- The Game Changers (Netflix)
- What The Health (YouTube)
- Forks Over Knives (YouTube)
- The End of Meat (YouTube)
- Meat Me Halfway (YouTube/ Amazon Prime)
- Eating Our Way to Extinction (Amazon Prime)
- The Invisible Vegan (Amazon Prime)
- The Animal People (Amazon Prime)
- A Prayer for Compassion (Amazon Prime)
- My Octopus Teacher (Netflix)
- Okja (Netflix)

My Top Pic: Babe / Babe: Pig in the City (Amazon or Netflix)

BOOKS

CLASSIC READS:

- **Vegetable Diet: As Sanctioned by Medical Men, and by Experience in All Ages (1838) by William A Alcott**: The world's first book to advocate a vegetarian diet! It's been reprinted by The American Antiquarian Cookbook Collection and still in print today.

- **Diet for a Small Planet (1971) by Frances Moore Lappe**: A groundbreaking book arguing that world hunger is caused by the meat industry. It was the first time that meat was shown to be unhealthy and leading to global poverty.

- **Animal Liberation (1975) by Peter Singer**: This book is widely considered the founding philosophical statement of its ideas within the animal liberation movement. Singer claimed that industrial farming is responsible for more pain and misery than all the wars of history put together.

- **Main Street Vegan: Everything You Need to Know to Eat Healthfully and Live Compassionately in the Real World (2012) by Victoria Moran**: Holistic health practitioner Victoria Moran offers a complete guide to making this dietary and lifestyle shift with an emphasis on practical "baby steps," proving that you don't have to have a personal chef or lifestyle coach on speed dial to experience the physical and spiritual benefits of being a vegan.

- **The China study: The Most Comprehensive Study of Nutrition Ever Conducted and the Startling Implications for Diet, Weight Loss and Long-Term Health (2004) by T. Colin Cambell**: This novel takes the reader through a twenty-year study which looked at mortality rates from cancer and other chronic diseases from 1973 to 1975 in 65 counties in China. The China Study examines the link between the consumption of animal products (including dairy) and chronic illnesses such as coronary heart disease, diabetes, breast cancer, prostate cancer, and bowel cancer.

MODERN READS:

- **Why We Love Dogs, Eat Pigs, and Wear Cows by Melanie Joy**: The social psychologist who coined the word and hidden belief system of "carnism." (Her YouTube channel is good as well).

- **Beyond Beliefs: A Guide to Improving Relationships and Communication for Vegans, Vegetarians, and Meat Eaters by Melanie Joy, PhD**: This book is recommended for anyone living with or in close relationships with non-vegans.

- **We Are the Weather: Saving the Planet Begins at Breakfast by Jonathon Safran Foer**: This book explains how collective human action is the only way to save the planet, and as the title suggests, this begins with what is on our plates.

- **Eating Animals by Jonathon Safran Foer**: Part memoir, part investigative report. This book is a moral examination of vegetarianism, farming, and the food we eat.

- **Sex Robots & Vegan Meat: Adventures at the Frontier of Birth, Food, Sex, and Death by Jenny Kleeman**: This novel is an investigation into the forces driving innovation in the core areas of human experience.

- **Some We Love, Some We Eat, Some We Hate: Why It's So Hard to Think Straight About Animals by Hal Herzog**: A scientist in the field of anthrozoology offers a controversial exploration of the psychology behind the ways we think, feel, and behave towards animals.

***ALL RESTAURANTS, APPLICATIONS, WEBSITES, AND OTHER RESOURCES ARE UP TO DATE AS OF THE TIME OF PUBLISHING.

TIMES ARE TURBULENT, AND THEREFORE DYNAMIC. ALWAYS DOUBLE CHECK TO ENSURE ORGANIZATIONS ARE STILL IN OPERATION.

ACKNOWLEDGMENTS

Although this travel guide is the final release in the Rebel Vegan trilogy, it was the original idea I developed and started writing during that first lonely lockdown. Bringing together my two great passions of travel and veganism kept me sane during those days of isolation.

First off, I could not have completed any of my books without the calm and steady stewardship of my trusted editor Gareth Clegg. He had faith in my vision and made it a reality. Thank you for believing in this book and me from the beginning.

My brilliant copywriter, Elaine Hutchison, proved invaluable in bringing this book to life. In the end, she absorbed more responsibility, kept me focused, and helped finish writing the book. She became a kindred spirit, and I look forward to writing together again. Thank you.

I am also grateful to my talented friend Alexandra in Chicago. She helped me research, write, and understand the vegan scene in North America and has always supported my vision.

As always, I am indebted to my talented design team: Marco, for designing my logo, Jelena for bringing my book cover concept to life, and my dear neighbor Cathy for her illustrations that open each chapter with a bold statement.

My assistant Ruth keeps me connected even when I am hiding away from the world and writing. Thank you for being my representative on earth.

For this book, I needed to go back and research my original struggles and triumphs while traveling. It was incredible to relive my first travels around the world—that first train journey down the boot of Italy. I had no cloud to store my stories or snapshots, so I relied on family for photos and memories. Back in my homeland of Canada, My Aunt Joan and my mother spent days digging out old letters and photographs from my original forays into the world.

And thanks to my dear friend Ann Rowley in Mexico. She forgets nothing, always has great stories, and opened up her photo album to me.

I feel exceptionally blessed and grateful to my dear friends. Knowing I had them in my corner gave me the confidence to go out into the world—and always brought me back again. Charlie and Jason have been two of my biggest supporters and kept me going during the long days of lockdown. My oldest friend, Rachael, has never faltered in her faith in me. Yodé and Osaro gave me a foothold in London and changed the course of my life. I love you all.

I am eternally grateful to Emma, who gave me strength and guidance at every step of this journey. We traveled around the world together, and I haven't stopped since. But I know I always have a home with you. Thank you for supporting and helping me find my way during these dark times.

And I can't forget my old partner-in-crime, Emma Fry. In 2009, She trained me on leading trips around South America and changed my life forever. She was also the first vegan in my life, and although it took a few years and a major illness, I caught up eventually. Thanks for your patience and incredible support through the years.

No matter how far I wandered, I was never lost as I knew I had strong roots. Thanks to my family, especially my parents, who gave me the confidence and support to go out into the world and find my way home again.

Finally, I am grateful beyond language for the incredible inspiration and guidance I have received from strangers throughout my travels.

**Your generosities restored my faith in humanity
and made me want to be a better person.**
This book is for you.

ABOUT THE AUTHOR

TODD SINCLAIR is the author of the *REBEL VEGAN LIFE* series.

A passionate travel expert, activist, podcaster, writer & speaker for the vegan cause, Todd currently lives his best *REBEL VEGAN LIFE* based in London.

If not writing in his favorite city, you can find him exploring the world—perfecting his cooking in Southeast Asia, trekking volcanoes, or scuba diving, all while promoting plant-based living and putting veganism on the map.

Find out more about *REBEL VEGAN* at the website
RebelVeganLife.com

Or on Social Media

facebook.com/RebelVeganLife
instagram.com/RebelVeganLife

ALSO BY TODD SINCLAIR

**REBEL VEGAN LIFE:
A RADICAL TAKE ON VEGANISM FOR A BRAVE NEW WORLD**

———————

**REBEL VEGAN LIFE:
A PLANT-BASED NUTRITION & BEGINNERS GUIDE**

———————

**REBEL VEGAN TRAVEL GUIDE:
VEGANISM ON THE GO**

REFERENCE NOTES

INTRODUCTION

1   Sustainable tourism .:. Sustainable Development Knowledge Platform (un.org)
2   Vegan Statistics | Veganism Around the World (vegansociety.com)
3   a food-borne pathogen from bacteria in meat.

1 - HIDDEN HISTORIES

1   Fad diet - Wikipedia
2   World History of Vegetarianism | The Vegetarian Society (vegsoc.org)
3   11 Most Famous Vegans in History - Powered by Orange
4   Extracts from some journals 1842-48—the earliest known uses of the word "vegetarian",
    http://www.ivu. org/history/vegetarian.html, accessed, 6th March 2012)
5   Leslie Cross Source Materials (candidhominid.com)- 50
    When Did Veganism Start? A Brief History Of The Vegan Movement - EcoPanda™ UK
    (myecopanda.com)- 25
    From imported document Vegetarian Guide: History of Vegetarianism in the U.S.
    (michaelbluejay.com) History | The Vegan Society
6   https://www.all-creatures.org/quotes/pythagoras.html
7   Vegetarianism and Religion (drexel.edu)
8   https://www.livekindly.co/history-veganism-around-world/
9   Vegetarianism in India: From Ancient to Modern Times (theflamingvegan.com)
    Do the Vedic literature allow meat-eating? Did Hinduism adopt vegetarianism from Buddhism?
    | The Spiritual Scientist
10 History of Vegetarianism - China & Vegetarianism (ivu.org)
11 The Hidden History of Greco-Roman Vegetarianism | Saving Earth | Encyclopedia Britannica
12 Livity (spiritual concept) - Wikipedia
13 Why Eating Meat Was Banned in Japan for Centuries - Gastro Obscura (atlasobscura.com)
    Vegan in Japan: Lessons Learned and Mistakes to Avoid (thenomadicvegan.com)
14 Here's Why Animal Liberation Has Ballooned in Jewish Culture | PETA
    How Israel Became the Global Center of Veganism - The Tower - The Tower
15 A Brief History of Veganism | Time
16 Ephrata Cloister - Wikipedia
17 British Dietetic Association confirms well-planned vegan diets can support healthy living in
    people of all ages | British Dietetic Association (BDA) for BDA. Get source for ADA and DOC
18 Bentham travel box: Auto-Icon | Bentham Project - UCL – University College London
19 Who were the world's very earliest vegans? | The Independent | The Independent
    Meat and Your Health | Animals Are Not Ours to Eat | PETA UK
20 The Evolution of Diet - National Geographic
21 https://www.worldveganorganisation.org/History/WorldVeganism
22 https://americanart.si.edu/artwork/nothing-else-worldnot-all-armiesis-so-powerful-idea-
    whose-time-has-come-victor-hugo-future
23 Veganism: A Decade in Review - The Veganary
24 Veganism - Wikipedia
25 Why More People Are Eating Plant-Based Protein During COVID-19 (healthline.com)
    After coronavirus: Our relationship with meat and the next pandemic | Environment | All
    topics from climate change to conservation | DW | 20.11.2020
26 Wet markets selling wildlife – birds, monkeys, bats and more – go quiet in Indonesia amid
    coronavirus pandemic | South China Morning Post (scmp.com)
27 https://www.nytimes.com/2020/04/13/opinion/animal-cruelty-coronavirus.html
28 Blue Zones sources:quotes only, find one for 9 characteristics https://www.nytimes.
    com/2012/10/28/magazine/the-island-where-people-forget-to-die.html
    https://www.nationalgeographic.com/magazine/article/these-traditional-diets-from-the-blue-
    zones-can-lead-to-long-lives-feature
    https://www.mayoclinic.org/healthy-lifestyle/nutrition-and-healthy-eating/in-depth/
    mediterranean-diet/art-20047801
29 Vegan Statistics | Veganism Around the World (vegansociety.com)
    30 Essential Vegan Statistics for a Healthier Life [Data for 2022] (dealsonhealth.net)

2 - A CAUTIONARY TALE

1   https://www.nationalgeographic.com/travel/article/heres-how-covid-is-changing-travel-according-to-the-experts
    https://www.impacttravelalliance.org/supporting-locals-from-home/
    https://www.nytimes.com/2020/07/02/travel/venice-coronavirus-tourism.html
    https://www.impacttravelalliance.org/supporting-locals-from-home/
    https://beunsettled.co/global-passport/
    https://www.impacttravelalliance.org/what-is-sustainable-tourism-everything-you-need-to-know-about-traveling-with-impact/
2   https://www.goodhousekeeping.com/life/g25383377/quotes-about-change/?slide=3
3   https://www.localtravelmovement.com/1201/local-travel-quotes/
4   p2_Black_Activist_Bios_FINAL.pdf (peta.org) source for below
    7 Social Justice Leaders You Never Knew Were Veg - ChooseVeg
5   Travel and tourism: share of global GDP 2020 | Statista How The Travel Industry Is Responding To The Rising Demand For Vegan Vacations (forbes.com)
6   Global Tourism Sees Upturn in Q3 but Recovery Remains Fragile (unwto.org)
7   The Most—and Least—Eco-Friendly Ways to Travel (afar.com)
    10 Easy Tips for Sustainable Tourism in Europe | Alternative Travelers
    What is Sustainable Travel & How to Travel Better | Charlie on Travel
8   https://ecotourism-world.com/quotes-about-ecotourism/
9   As the pandemic prompts eco-awareness, the travel industry responds - The Washington Post
10 United Airlines agrees to purchase 15 supersonic aircrafts | abc10.com
    British Airways-owner IAG to cut emissions with sustainable aviation fuel target | Reuters
1   https://www.goodreads.com/quotes/87476-a-goal-without-a-plan-is-just-a-wish
2   https://www.qualtrics.com/blog/research-quotes/

3 - PLANNING AND PACKING

3   https://www.thenomadicvegan.com/vegan-apps-for-travelers/
4   https://chrome.google.com/webstore/detail/growbot-automator-for-ins/abhcgokmndbiegmmbjffdlpihgdmeejf?hl=en
5   https://theveganword.com/packing-vegan-suitcase/ https://www.strongsuitcases.com/blogs/news/the-ultimate-vegan-friendly-packing-checklist
    https://www.livekindly.co/7-vegan-carry-on-luggage-travel-essentials-for-your-next-vacation/
6   https://www.203challenges.com/15-packing-quotes-to-help-you-travel-light/
7   https://www.insidethetravellab.com/you-coronavirus-packing-list-what-to-pack-for-travel-during-the-covid-outbreak/
8   https://www.203challenges.com/15-packing-quotes-to-help-you-travel-light/

4 - REBEL VEGAN TOUR

1   https://chainomad.com/eating-vegan-in-india/
    https://www.indianholiday.com/blog/eating-vegan-dishes-in-india/
2   https://www.thenomadicvegan.com/vegan-in-peru/
    https://www.thenomadicvegan.com/vegan-restaurants-cusco-peruvian-chocolate/
    https://www.livinginperu.com/5-reasons-peru-is-vegan-friendly-plus-where-to-eat/
3   https://www.theveganary.com/taiwan/
    https://www.theveganary.com/vegan-street-food-in-taiwan/
4   https://positivelypancakes.blogspot.com/2016/01/my-top-10-vegan-restaurants-in-australia.html
    https://www.thenomadicvegan.com/vegan-in-australia/
    https://www.vegantravel.com/destinations/oceania/australia/
    Ultimate Guide to Being Vegan in Australia | The Nomadic Vegan
5   https://veganswithappetites.com/eating-vegan-in-thailand/
    https://thailandforme.com/the-vegetarian-vegans-guide-to-eating-in-tAs hailand/
    Top Tips for A Vegan in Thailand | The Nomadic Vegan
6   https://www.livekindly.co/7-tips-travelling-vegan-indonesia/
    https://www.theveganary.com/indonesia/
    https://www.bemytravelmuse.com/vegan-indonesia/
7   https://www.thenomadicvegan.com/vegan-in-japan/
    https://www.justhungry.com/japan-dining-out-cards
    https://the-shooting-star.com/japan-vegan-vegetarian-survival-guide/
8   https://jessicainthekitchen.com/tips-for-eating-vegetarian-or-vegan-in-jamaica/
    https://theculturetrip.com/caribbean/jamaica/articles/a-vegan-guide-to-jamaica/
    https://www.vegantravel.com/destinations/north-america/caribbean/jamaica/
9   https://vegconomist.com/studies-and-numbers/study-new-zealand-is-now-the-fifth-most-vegan-country-in-the-world/
    https://www.vegansociety.org.nz/resources/eatingout/nz-map
    https://forgoodnessseyks.com/vegantravelnewzealand/

10 https://happyherbivore.com/2014/07/vegan-portugal-lisbon-cascais/
    https://www.thetastyk.com/2018/12/17/vegan-in-portugal/
    https://www.portugalholidays4u.com/articles/eating-vegan-in-portugal
11 https://costaricatravelblog.com/vegan-and-vegetarian-food-in-costa-rica/
    https://mytanfeet.com/costa-rican-food/vegan-vegetarian-costa-rica/
    https://www.thatwasvegan.com/2019/09/17/amazing-vegan-food-in-costa-rica/
12 https://thenomadicvegan.com/vegan-italy/
    https://www.eatingeurope.com/blog/vegan-italy/
    https://www.intrepidtravel.com/adventures/italy-for-vegan-travellers/
13 https://www.intrepidtravel.com/adventures/vegan-vegetarian-gluten-free-vietnam/
    https://www.thenomadicvegan.com/vegan-vietnam-tour-package/
    https://veggievagabonds.com/vegan-in-vietnam-vegan-guide/
    https://www.veganfoodquest.com/vegan-guide-to-vietnam/
14 https://veganinireland.com/is-ireland-vegan-friendly
    https://veganinireland.com/planning-and-organizing-your-vegan-irish-trip
    https://www.veganvstravel.com/2019/03/vegan-ireland.html
    https://vagabondtoursofireland.com/eating-vegetarian-in-ireland
15 https://www.vegansociety.com/news/blog/10-ways-eat-vegan-greece
    https://www.thenomadicvegan.com/the-nomadic-vegans-guide-to-greece/
    https://www.thenomadicvegan.com/greece-vegan-travel/
    https://www.lemonsandluggage.com/locals-honest-guide-being-vegan-in-greece/

5 - REBEL VEGAN CITY TOUR

1   http://www.veganamsterdam.org/
2   https://www.solosophie.com/quotes-about-amsterdam/
3   The Most Vegan-Friendly Caribbean Islands - Veggies Abroad Vegan Travel
4   https://www.inspiringquotes.us/author/8142-rihanna
5   The Vegan Adventure - Vegan Travel Guides, Current Events and More: Traveling Vegan:
    Austin, TX
6   https://oklahomawonders.com/best-quotes-about-austin-texas-for-austin-instagram-
    captions-status/
7   https://theveganary.com/germany/
    https://fearlessfemaletravels.com/eating-vegetarian-in-germany/
    https://www.alternativetravelers.com/berlin-vegan-guide/
8   https://www.veganvstravel.com/2017/10/best-places-to-eat-out-in-budapest.html
9   https://mylittlehungary.com/inspiring-quotes-about-budapest/
10 https://www.veganvstravel.com/2017/10/best-places-to-eat-out-in-budapest.html
11 https://www.wisefamousquotes.com/quotes-about-buenos-aires/
12 Vegan Guide to Cairo, Egypt - Vegan Travel Blog on VeganTravel.com
13 https://www.goodreads.com/quotes/tag/cairo
14 https://travel.usnews.com/Cape_Town_South_Africa/
15 https://www.veganfriendly.org.uk/articles/festivals-and-events/
    https://theveganword.com/vegan-london-travel-guide/
    https://www.veganlondon.co.uk/
16 Vegan Morocco Travel Tips: What to Eat | Nomadic Vegan (thenomadicvegan.com)
17 https://www.goodreads.com/quotes/tag/marrakech
18 https://madridvegantravel.com/
19 https://www.wisesayings.com/madrid-quotes/
20 https://theveganword.com/vegan-paris/
    https://www.thenomadicvegan.com/vegan-paris/
21 https://www.alternativetravelers.com/cheap-vegan-food-portland/
    https://www.happycow.net/blog/portland-vegfest-2015-tips-and-highlights/
22 https://www.theguardian.com/travel/2007/dec/15/portlandusa.usa
23 https://www.veggievisa.com/vegan-travel-prague-czech-republic/
24 https://historyfangirl.com/quotes-about-prague-captions-statuses/
25 Eating Vegan in Puerto Vallarta, Mexico - Vegan Travel Blog on VeganTravel.com
    Conde Nast Travelers rank Puerto Vallarta among "The Best Cities in the World"
    (vallartadaily.com)
26 About Puerto Vallarta: Attractions & History | Vallarta Adventures (vallarta-adventures.com)
27 https://www.susgain.com/blog/how-to-find-affordable-vegan-and-vegetarian-options-in-
    singapore/
    https://plantbasednews.org/opinion/travel-a-vegans-guide-to-singapore/
28 https://www.timeout.com/singapore/things-to-do/famous-quotes-about-singapore-that-sum-
    up-our-city
29 https://igoogleisrael.com/now-this-is-why-every-vegan-should-be-visiting-tel-aviv/
    https://vegan-friendly.co.il/
30 Vegan Guide to Toronto – Vegan Travel Eats
    Toronto Now Has Its Own Vegan Neighborhood - Welcome to Vegandale (livekindly.co)

31 https://www.inspiringquotes.us/topic/5119-toronto
32 http://www.vildamagazine.com/2019/01/vegan-guide-to-vienna/
    https://veganonboard.com/where-to-find-the-best-vegan-food-in-vienna/
33 http://brightnomad.net/vegan-travel-warsaw-poland/
    https://veganswithappetites.com/eating-vegan-in-warsaw-poland/

34 https://libquotes.com/winston-churchill/quote/lbp8v6g

6 - STAYCATIONS

1   How staycation became a new trend in COVID-times - The Financial Express
2   https://www.virtuoso.com/travel/articles/10-international-travel-quotes-to-motivate-you
3   STAYCATION English Definition and Meaning | Lexico.com
4   http://innonthedrive.com/what-is-a-staycation-and-why-you-need-one/
    https://www.businessinsider.com/safe-vacations-during-covid?op=1
5   https://www.goodhousekeeping.com/life/travel/g30549533/staycation-ideas/
    https://www.parents.com/fun/vacation/ideas/staycation-ideas-for-spring-break/

7 - CONNECTIONS

1   Most Die-Hard Vegetarians Are Actually Pretty Wishy-Washy (vice.com)
2   https://www.travelandleisure.com/travel-tips/celebrity-travel/anthony-bourdain-travel-
    food-quotes
3   New Study Reveals 84% of Vegetarians Return to Meat (sciencealert.com)
4   Maslow's Hierarchy of Needs | Simply Psychology
5   https://www.pappaspost.com/remembering-stamatis-moraitis-man-who-almost-forgot-die/
    https://www.nytimes.com/2012/10/28/magazine/the-island-where-people-forget-to-die.html
    https://www.theguardian.com/world/2013/may/31/ikaria-greece-longevity-secrets-age

8 - BUMPS IN THE ROAD

1   https://www.peta.org/living/entertainment/vegan-friendly-websites-to-help-you-plan-
    the-perfect-vacation/
    https://www.theveganhopper.com/en/the-challenges-of-vegan-travel-and-how-to-deal-
    with-them/
    https://www.dontforgettomove.com/traveling-as-a-vegetarian/
    https://www.washingtonpost.com/lifestyle/travel/can-you-maintain-a-vegan-diet-while-
    traveling-yes-but-it-will-take-some-strategizing/2016/03/29/19e08b68-ebbc-11e5-bc08-
    3e03a5b41910_story.html
    What Countries are Cruel to Animals in 2021? - Cruelty Free Soul
    How to Help Stop Animal Abuse in the Tourism Industry (nomadicmatt.com)

9 - FINAL DESTINATION

1   https://www.inc.com/larry-kim/19-short-inspirational-quotes-for-overcoming-adversity.html

10 - VEGAN TRAVEL RECIPES

1   Veganuniversal.com source for txt box - www.un.org - peta.org
    https://www.goodreads.com/quotes/13287-you-see-things-you-say-why-but-i-dream-things

CPSIA information can be obtained
at www.ICGtesting.com
Printed in the USA
BVHW010818170223
658731BV00006B/433